Realm Crafter User's Guide

First Edition

Covers Realm Crafter v1.26

By Frank Succardi

Copyright 2015

Realm Crafter User's Guide

By: Frank Succardi

Cover Art: Frank Succardi

Copyright © 2015 Frank Succardi

All rights reserved.

This book may not be reproduced in whole or in part, by any means now known or yet to be invented, without the express written permission of the Copyright Owner, excepting brief quotes used in reviews or scholarly journals. The purchase of a copy of this book does not confer upon the purchaser license to use this work or any part therein in other works, including derivatives.

Every effort had been made in the preparation of this book to ensure the accuracy of the information presented herein. The information contained within this book is sold without warranty, neither express nor implied. The Author will not be held liable for any damages caused or alleged to be caused directly or indirectly by this book.

All commercial trademarks are the exclusive property of the trademark holder.

Realm Crafter is a registered trademark of Solstar, Incorporated.

ISBN #: 978-1-312-40578-3

Frank Succardi
Santa Fe, NM 87508
USA

More Info: realmcrafterbook@franksuccardi.com

Table of Contents

About the Author — i

Dedication — ii

Acknowledgements — iii

Preface — iv

Introduction — viii

    Why I Wrote This Book — viii

    Who This Book Is For — ix

    What You Need For This Book — xi

    Tools of the Trade — xiii

    Media Formats Supported — xiii

    A Note About Licensing — xv

Chapter 1: RCS Project Manager — 1

    Projects Tab — 2

    Toolbox Tab — 3

Chapter 2: RCS Game Editor — 6

Chapter 3: Project Tab — 10

    Project Tab Details — 10

    Build Full Client — 11

    Generate Client Update — 11

Table of Contents

BUILD FULL SERVER	12
Chapter 4: Media Tab	**13**
MEDIA TAB DETAILS	13
MEDIA LIBRARY VIEW SELECTION LIST	14
ADD NEW FILE	15
ADDING 3D MESHES	15
3D FILE FORMATS SUPPORTED	15
ADDING TEXTURES	16
TEXTURE FILE FORMATS SUPPORTED	16
ADDING SOUNDS	18
SOUND / AUDIO FORMATS SUPPORTED	18
ADDING MUSIC	18
MUSIC FORMATS SUPPORTED	18
REMOVE FILE	19
FOLDER NAVIGATOR	19
FILE SELECTOR	19
MEDIA PREVIEW WINDOW	19
INITIAL SCALE (IN 3D MESH SELECTION ONLY)	19
Chapter 5: Particles Tab	**20**
PARTICLES TAB DETAILS	20

Table of Contents

PARTICLE PREVIEW WINDOW	20
ACTIVE PARTICLES	20
PREVIEW TEXTURE	21
RESET PREVIEW	21
PREVIEW ADJUSTMENT CONTROLS	21
CURRENT EMITTER SELECTION LIST	21
NEW EMITTER	21
SAVE EMITTERS	21
DELETE EMITTER	21
GENERAL SETTINGS TAB	22
COLORING TAB	24
ANIMATED TEXTURE OPTIONS	26
SHAPE OPTIONS	27
VELOCITY TAB	29
FORCES TAB	31
SAMPLE PARTICLE	32
Chapter 6: Combat Tab	**34**
COMBAT TAB DETAILS	34
SAVE DAMAGE TYPES	34
LIST OF DAMAGE TYPES	34

Table of Contents

    Combat Options 35

Chapter 7: Projectiles Tab — 38

    Projectiles Tab Details 38

    Managing the Projectiles List 38

    Projectile Properties 39

Chapter 8: Factions Tab — 41

    Factions Tab Details 41

    Managing the Factions List 43

    Adjusting Faction Ratings 44

Chapter 9: Animations Tab — 45

    Animations Tab Details 45

    Managing Animation Sets 46

    Animation Set Properties 46

Chapter 10: Attributes Tab — 48

    Attributes Tab Details 48

    Managing the Attributes List 49

    Set Fixed Attributes 49

    Attribute is a Skill Option 50

    Hide Attribute From Players Option 50

    Assignable Attribute Points Available at Character Creation 50

Table of Contents

Chapter 11: Actors Tab — 51

- Actors Tab Details — 51
- Managing the Actors List — 52
- Actor Properties — 52
- Description Tab — 53
- General Tab — 55
- Appearance Tab — 58
- Starting Gear — 61
- Attributes Tab — 64
- Preview Tab — 66

Chapter 12: Items Tab — 67

- Items Tab Details — 67
- Managing the Items List — 67
- General Tab — 69
- Specific Tab — 70
- Weapon Specifics — 71
- Armor Specifics — 73
- Ring Specifics — 73
- Potion Specifics — 74
- Food Specifics — 75

Table of Contents

IMAGE SPECIFICS 76

OTHER SPECIFICS 77

APPEARANCE TAB 78

ATTRIBUTES TAB 79

OTHER TAB 81

Chapter 13: Days & Seasons Tab — 83

DAYS & SEASONS TAB DETAILS 83

SAVE SETTINGS 83

GENERAL 84

MONTHS 84

SEASONS 84

SUNS & MOONS 85

Chapter 14: Zones Tab — 88

ZONES TAB DETAILS 88

ZONE MANAGEMENT 89

ZONE PREVIEW WINDOW 90

SELECT 90

MOVE 90

ROTATE 91

SCALE 91

Table of Contents

Precise — 92

Camera Speed — 92

X, Y, Z Camera Coordinates — 93

Moving the Camera — 93

Mode Selection Buttons — 94

Zone Editing Mode Button Details — 94

Zone Editing Mode Button Details (continued) — 95

Scenery Mode — 96

Terrain Mode — 99

Emitters Mode — 101

Water Mode — 102

Collision Box Mode — 104

Sound Zone Mode — 105

Trigger Zone Mode — 108

Waypoint Mode — 110

Portal Mode — 113

Environment Options — 115

Other Options — 121

Chapter 15: Abilities Tab — **124**

Abilities Tab Details — 124

Table of Contents

MANAGING ABILITIES	125
ABILITY PROPERTIES	125

Chapter 16: Interface Tab   127

INTERFACE TAB DETAILS	127

Chapter 17: Other Tab   130

OTHER TAB DETAILS	130

Chapter 18: RCS Game Client   135

UPDATES	136
CLIENT DETAILS	137
GRAPHICS OPTIONS	139
CONTROL OPTIONS	141
OTHER OPTIONS	142
CHARACTER SELECTION SCREEN	142
CREATING A NEW CHARACTER	144
CHARACTER WINDOW	144
ATTRIBUTES WINDOW	145
NAME WINDOW	145
GAME CLIENT MAIN SCREEN	146
GAME TOOLBAR	147
INVENTORY	148

ABILITIES	149
CHARACTER SHEET	150
QUEST JOURNAL	151
SAMPLE QUEST SCRIPT	152
CONTROLLING THE GAME	156
TRADING	156
FORMING A PARTY	156
IN-GAME COMMANDS	157
Chapter 19: Customizing the Client	**161**
LOCALIZING AND CUSTOMIZING THE CLIENT LANGUAGE	161
CUSTOMIZING THE ACTION BAR	161
CUSTOMIZING THE CLIENT LAYER	162
CUSTOMIZING THE COMPASS	162
CUSTOMIZING THE STATUS BARS	162
CUSTOMIZING THE INVENTORY WINDOW	162
THE INVENTORY BACKGROUND IS LOCATED AT:	162
CUSTOMIZING THE ABILITIES WINDOW	162
CUSTOMIZING THE CHARACTER WINDOW	163
CUSTOMIZING THE QUEST JOURNAL WINDOW	163
CUSTOMIZING THE PARTY WINDOW	163

Table of Contents

    CUSTOMIZING THE HELP WINDOW   163

Chapter 20: The Game Server   **164**

    SERVER ACCOUNTS WINDOW   165

    SERVER GAME STATUS WINDOW   166

    SERVER UPDATES WINDOW   169

    DEPLOYING THE GAME SERVER AND UPDATES   171

    DEPLOYING GAME CLIENT UPDATES   175

Glossary   **179**

Appendix A: Updater Language.txt   **187**

About the Author

Frank Succardi is a freelance programmer, multimedia producer, and technology consultant. He is also Founder/CEO of a technology consulting firm serving businesses and government clients across the country.

With a heavy background in the independent study of video, audio, animation, programming, and game theory/design, along with a degree in Electronic Media, building MMORPG's seemed like a natural path to take.

As a college professor, Frank has taught accredited classes in 3D Studio, Multimedia Authoring, Interactive Programming, Introduction to Multimedia, Introduction to Computers, 2D Animation, and 3D Animation.

Frank was the Founder and President of the Santa Fe Gamers' Guild, and a long-standing member of the Realm Crafter Community; contributing to the Community Wiki, authoring multiple articles, guides, and tutorials, as well as answering questions for new users. Frank has also been part of the Realm Crafter development team for his work on program documentation.

His interests are gaming, programming, virtual reality, 3D visualization, science fiction, historical recreation, multimedia production, game design, and time off with his family and his beloved dogs.

Dedication

I dedicate this book to my mother, who wasn't always sure about what I was doing, but encouraged me anyway. Her creativity continues to inspire me.

Acknowledgements

I want to thank my beautiful wife Brandie, without whose patience, love, and support this book would never have become a reality.

I also like to thank the following contributors:

Atu'los

Ben J

Jason G

Timothy C

Of course, I'd also like to thank the supportive Realm Crafter community, and Dragon, for giving me this opportunity.

Preface

I remember the first time I played an RPG just as if it was yesterday. It was 1980; I was 12 years old and had just moved from an inner city on the east coast to a rural area in a state in the southwest. There was not much for kids to do, so I found myself hanging out at the local independent toy store. The store had everything from puppets, to science toys, to books. On one of the book displays, mixed up with "How to Draw..." books, I ran across a set of books that caught my eye: Advanced Dungeons and Dragons. I looked through the books and was very interested with the idea of a fantasy story-telling game. The charts and text were very complex and I didn't really understand it at first. I asked some friends at school about AD&D and they invited me to come and play. I was instantly hooked.

In the years that followed, I played so many different RPG's I can hardly remember them all. There were Champions, Top Secret, Gamma World, Paranoia, Shadowrun, Morrow Project, Traveller, and more. It seemed like there were always people who wanted to play, but not many that wanted to do the work of coming up with scenarios, learning the rules, and hosting. I mostly did the work of the GM, but I didn't mind. I had so many hours of fun, building friendships with other players, contributing to group-generated stories that evolved over time, and exercising creativity in fantastical, heroic, or absurd situations with friends. We still talk about epic, noteworthy stories from our games with a sense of fondness and nostalgia.

Our stories and adventures surpassed anything we had ever read or any movie we had ever seen, or any story we ever heard because *we* made them up, collectively, out of our own imaginations. Through this story-telling medium we also accidentally learned about math, statistics, probability, plot structures, creative writing, character development, plot devices, mood, foreshadowing, performance art, first aid, strategy, history, spontaneity, and improvisation.

Unfortunately, life can get in the way of fun; people grow apart, go off to college, take time to build families, or move away in search of love or a good paying job. The hectic pace of adult life means we have less and less time to spend in the realm of imagination, being creative with people whose company we enjoy, rolling dice, making up stories, and building fond memories.

During this time, computers were not very advanced. The first adventure games that came out were text-based, or had very basic graphics. My first computer RPG was Temple of Apshai in 1980. Each room had an on-screen number that corresponded with descriptions you had to look up in a book, and the graphics were horrible.

Electronic role playing was extremely limited. Games like Zork and Suspended were very popular, but due to the very simple nature of the game technology, people became bored and frustrated with what amounted to a guessing game of what word combinations the game would respond to.

After text-based games came titles that were a little more advanced, but had no multiplayer aspect. Games like Ultima allowed you to form a group of adventurers and guide them through an online world, but were still a single-player game. Later, games like Dungeon offered better graphics and game mechanics, but were still somewhat dull, single-player games. Multiplayer games were just in their infancy, with titles like MULE, which allowed up to four players to compete for resources on an alien planet.

Over time, the Internet was invented, and with that came text based, distributed, multiplayer games, called MUD's (Multi User Dungeons or Dimensions). Games like MUME (Multi User Middle Earth) and Multitrek became very popular with college and university students who could use Unix-based workstations (or any workstation that supported VT100 terminal emulation) to tap into these games.

Soon after came the most well known, true MMORPG: EverQuest. The graphics were nothing to write home about, but they were very decent; far better than anything we had seen up to that point. EverQuest became quite popular and was followed by a second edition (EverQuest 2), and more MMORPG's, such as Horizons, and World of Warcraft.

Thankfully, technology has progressed to the point that distance and time don't matter so much. Distance can be conquered through online tabletop game simulation and teleconferencing, or through MMORPG's; many of which are either free or very inexpensive to play.

All along, I had been searching for a way to make my game ideas accessible to the public. I wanted to recapture that old-school gaming feel, but with modern technology. I tried adapting 3D engines, which was a lot of work. I found a decent platform in the NeverWinter Nights Aurora authoring system. Unfortunately, it had a restrictive licensing scheme and was limited to the d20 system only, so it

Preface

wasn't very flexible as an MMORPG authoring tool. However, I did like the way people could link their worlds together and to produce their own adventures with relative ease.

Eventually, a friend of mine heard about Realm Crafter and sent me a link to their web site. This was exactly what I was looking for. Realm Crafter featured a decent 3D engine, a good licensing scheme, an authoring system, a scripting engine, server, updater, inexpensive authoring platform, and more. This is the product I would use to create my own MMORPG.

The RC Standard program was still in development, and had terrible documentation, along with a lot of bugs and things that may not have been fully thought out. However, the developer seemed responsive to customer requests for features, and although they were slow to deliver upgrades, updates, and patches, they were still an easy to use, decent quality authoring system for MMORPG's. Plans were made and development started on a Pro version of Realm Crafter. It had a better development interface, more features, a better programming interface, and support for DirectX9. It was shaping up into a very nice product. Unfortunately, progress on development stalled and sputtered, then stopped completely.

At the time of this writing, Realm Crafter Standard has been discontinued by Solstar, with existing users getting access to the source code. Is this the end of easy-to-use MMORPG creation software?

The good news is a stubborn group of hard-working and creative Realm Crafter enthusiasts have moved forward with the development of a Realm Crafter Community Edition. I will endeavor to continue providing quality documentation relevant to the Realm Crafter Community Edition.

There are also rumors of a new edition of Realm Crafter on the horizon. Solstar is currently advertising Realm Crafter: Resurrection. I will endeavor to keep the documentation relevant to future editions of the Realm Crafter line.

I look forward to the future of this type of product for independent developers and hobbyists, whatever form it may come in. There is a new generation of game developers just waiting for an opportunity to express their creativity, come up with the next great game mechanic, tell new stories, and maybe make a little money.

Preface

I hope this book serves to make MMORPG development more approachable for more people. It was my aim to make everything as clear and easy to understand as possible using plain, easy to understand English. I have avoided using technical terms as much as possible, and where it was unavoidable, I provided definitions in the Glossary.

Introduction

Why I Wrote This Book

I really like Realm Crafter. The possibilities are limitless. However, it was very hard to figure out how to work it. I was tired of the sparse documentation that came with the product. There were no details on how the server, updater, and client work together. Scouring the Forums took forever, and the Wikis were incomplete.

I wanted to have a User's Manual that I could reference on various Realm Crafter functions and topics. I set out to write a manual for myself, but then I realized such a manual would likely be helpful to other users, especially those just getting started in the industry, as well as those who just need the missing pieces they are looking for.

Introduction

It is my hope that this book will help make Realm Crafter Standard more accessible to people who are interested in MMORPG development, but who may have been put off by the restrictive license fees, royalty payments, expense, and complexity of other authoring systems.

Realm Crafter Standard has a lot of potential and could really be a great program for ambitious independent game developers; it just needs a little polish.

This is my contribution to that polish!

I hope you have as much fun reading this book as I had writing it. Please enjoy yourself expressing your imagination, creativity, and vision by creating fantastic virtual worlds with Realm Crafter Standard.

Who This Book Is For
This book is for anybody who is interested in advancing their knowledge of the Realm Crafter Standard product, especially those interested in creating their own multiplayer online role playing games of any genre.

Although anybody with an interest will find this book useful to a lesser or greater extent, it was written for users with little or no experience with game development.

Most of the readers of this book probably fall into one of the following categories:

Hobbyists - Many people like to tinker and dabble. Realm Crafter is great for creating your own virtual world that you can be constantly working on; upgrading and changing over time to suit the vision you have of your world.

If you have an idea for a good scenario, or just have a creative idea, you would like to play out or share with friends, Realm Crafter is a great way to create a sandbox environment for your friends and family to explore.

By adding to your world little by little, as you develop new ideas and new areas, you can grow your world over time.

Lone Wolf Producers - Many people have all the skills they need to produce their own multiplayer online game, but lack the advanced programming skills required for 3D graphics engines. This makes Realm Crafter the perfect product. By leveraging its inexpensive 3D graphics engine and very fair licensing, lone wolf producers can put together complete game worlds for commercial or non-profit purposes.

Introduction

Independent Production Boutiques / Small Teams - It is uncommon for hobbyists and lone wolves to possess all the skills needed to take a game from concept to delivery. It is much more common for small groups of people with diverse skills to come together on a project.

Realm Crafter's segmented approach allows multiple production areas to be developed simultaneously. This allows the project to be broken up into smaller, more manageable tasks, speeding up the development process.

Small production teams generally include the following staff structure, with some team members taking on one or more positions:

Writer- Responsible for coming up with ideas and writing stories and dialogs for the virtual world. The Writer creates all the body copy for the Quest descriptions and updates, along with all the NPC dialogs and even the System Messages. The Writer can also create ad copy and press-releases for promoting the game. The Writer must be familiar with using modern word processing software, should have a "way with words", be good at creative writing, and be able to communicate in a clear and professional manner. A good writer has attention to detail and checks for typos and bad grammar.

Programmer- Responsible for coding all the interactions and automatic behaviors of NPC's as well as automated housekeeping tasks. This includes spells, item interactions, effect timers, combat, and anything that happens automatically in the game world. The programmer needs to have a good grasp of programming techniques, be familiar with the RC BSL programming language, and be able to use either the built-in RC Script Editor or another text editor of choice, such as Notepad++ for editing scripts.

Graphic Artist- Responsible for designing the visual elements of the game. The Graphic Artist designs the style of the buildings, armor, weapons, buttons, icons, clothes, characters, monsters, and items. The Graphic Artist should be familiar with creating both 2D and 3D digital art using mainstream tools, as well as using traditional tools, such as pen and paper.

Creative Designer- Responsible for designing the game mechanics, coming up with ideas about how things work in the game world, defining how the combat system, skill progression, experience, and crafting system should work, as well as anything else having to do with game concepts.

Introduction

Audio Specialist- Responsible for music, sound effects, background environment sounds, and so forth.

Producer- Responsible for managing the team, getting bills paid, acquiring hardware and software, and making business decisions.

What You Need For This Book

This book is meant to be used as a supplement to existing Realm Crafter Standard documentation. In order to be successful with Realm Crafter, you need the following:

- Version 1.26 or higher of Realm Crafter Standard
- A computer that meets the minimum requirements to run Realm Crafter:
- **CPU Model:** Pentium 4 or higher
- **CPU Speed:** 1.3 GHz or faster
- **RAM:** 512 MB or more
- **Graphics Card:** GeForce 5500 or Radeon 9800 or better
- Graphics Memory: 128 MB or more
- **Graphics Protocol**: DirectX 7 or higher
- **Network Play:** By LAN or Internet
- **Operating System:** Windows 2000/XP/Vista or higher
- **Hard Drive:** Approx 300 MB of free space for Realm Crafter. Additional storage requirements depend on the size of the media files included in the project.

In addition to the hardware and software mentioned above, you should also possess as many of these traits as possible:

Patience - Taking your project from ideas to finished product can take a long time and requires loads of hard work and patience. You are likely to make mistakes and have false-starts along the way, so expect that to happen and don't get angry or discouraged when it does. When this happens, just take a break, walk around, listen to music, take a nap, play a game, read a book, or relax. The brain needs some time to process complex ideas and come up with solutions. You can't force the process to go faster, but you can facilitate the process by taking a break from the project and distracting your brain with a different topic for a while. Having simple toys to play with, or other small diversions helps pass the time and allows the brain to organize the new information and arrive at a conclusion more easily.

Introduction

Ideas - Being creative is all about expressing your ideas. You can use Realm Crafter as a way to visualize and interact with those ideas. Keep a notebook with you at all times, even if it is just the memo pad in your cell phone. As you go through your day, keep your mind open to interesting things you see around you. Maybe a newspaper article caught your eye. Maybe you just read some stories on mythology or science fiction. Maybe a good idea just came to you while you were spacing out. Keeping a notebook or voice recorder handy will help capture those ideas for further development. Don't be afraid to try something, even if it ends up not working out, you still had a learning experience, and that in itself is valuable.

Passion - Love of gaming, or tinkering, or building, or thinking, or being creative is what gives producers the drive to move their projects forward. This passion keeps game development constantly on their mind. Having the passion to pursue your ideas and dreams provides the drive to see your project to completion.

Willingness to Learn - Game production is a learning process. You learn what works and what doesn't, with respect to the idea you have and the way it can be presented by computer interface. A Producer must be open to learning lessons as they go through the production process. Realizing that nobody can know everything about everything will allow you to give yourself permission to take risks, push your comfort zone, learn lessons both good and bad, and adjust your course of actions. This experience is what contributes to your next project and allows you to look at issues with a more seasoned eye.

Tenacity - Don't give up! Tenacity works hand-in-hand with passion. While passion provides the drive to move forward, tenacity provides the ability to get back up, dust yourself off, and get back to work when failure seems frequent and forward progress seems impossible. Be stubborn; don't let obstacles trip you up. If you make a mistake, try to correct it and move on. If you lack the knowledge or skill to accomplish a task, then study it or find somebody who has those skills to help you. Every problem has at least one solution; they just aren't always obvious.

You will also need a toolkit of helper programs to create the media for your game:

Introduction

Tools of the Trade

Since Realm Crafter is an authoring system, almost all the media used in your project needs to be created in a 3rd party application of your choice and imported into the Master Media List through the Game Editor.

Media Formats Supported

Realm Crafter Standard is a very versatile program that allows for importing media in a variety of common formats.

Audio

Audio can be created and edited with any program that supports WAV, MP3, OGG, or RAW format.

3D Models

3D meshes can be created and edited with any program that supports B3D, EB3D, X, or 3DS format.

Animation

Animated models must be in B3D format and must use a bone structure compatible with Realm Crafter.

Bones required for animated players:

- Head
- L_Shoulder
- R_Shoulder
- Chest
- L_Forearm
- R_Forearm
- L_Shin
- R_Shin
- L_Hand
- R_Hand
- L_Foot
- R_Foot

Audio and Music

Audacity is available free online and supports MP3, WAV, and OGG formats. It features multitrack recording and its features rival those of commercial products.

Introduction

Acid Music Studio is a good, inexpensive commercial option that has a lot of pre-made loops, multitrack recording, and tons of support.

Animated 3D Models

Animated meshes must be in b3d format and must have at least one bone called "head".

Blender is a free 3D modeler and has a b3d exporter capable of creating animated meshes.

Fragmotion is a commercial product that imports most formats, allows rigging, and exports animated b3d format.

Static 3D Meshes

Blender is a free 3D modeler and supports 3DS, X, and B3D. It can export static (non-animated) meshes.

Milkshape is free and supports 3DS, X, and exports B3D.

Anim8or is free and exports 3DS files.

3dtin is free and works in your browser. It can export OBJ format, which can be converted to 3DS or B3D in most 3D programs, such as Blender.

3D Studio Max is great commercial software that exports 3DS and X formats. It is very expensive, but you may qualify for the free student edition, so see their web site for details.

Paint

GiMP is a great free program that rivals many commercial photo and art editing programs. There is a lot of online support for this program.

Vector

Inkscape is a free program that allows the creation of vector graphics. Realm Crafter doesn't use vectors directly, but vector art can be used in conjunction with other programs, such as to make paths for 3D extrusion.

A Note About Licensing

It is important to know and understand the licensing agreement for any third-party media you may use in your project. Most third-party vendors want you to protect their media, instead of giving it away with your project.

In these cases, you must use a program that protects sources, such as the commercial product MoleBox. This program keeps your source files hidden, so they cannot be directly viewed with a file browser

Chapter 1: RCS Project Manager

Figure 1.1 Project Manager Main Screen

Massive Multiplayer games tend to have many media assets. There could be hundreds or even thousands of graphics files, 3D meshes, sound effects, and music files. Each collection of related files represents a single Project.

Every Project needs to be created, edited, and managed. The RCS Project Manager is the tool to use to create new projects and to switch between the helper programs to develop, build, and detail your project.

It can also be useful to work between multiple projects. For example, you may have two projects; one project that you use as a "scratch pad" to test ideas, and the other to be the "final draft" or Production Project.

Chapter 1: RCS Project Manager

Projects Tab

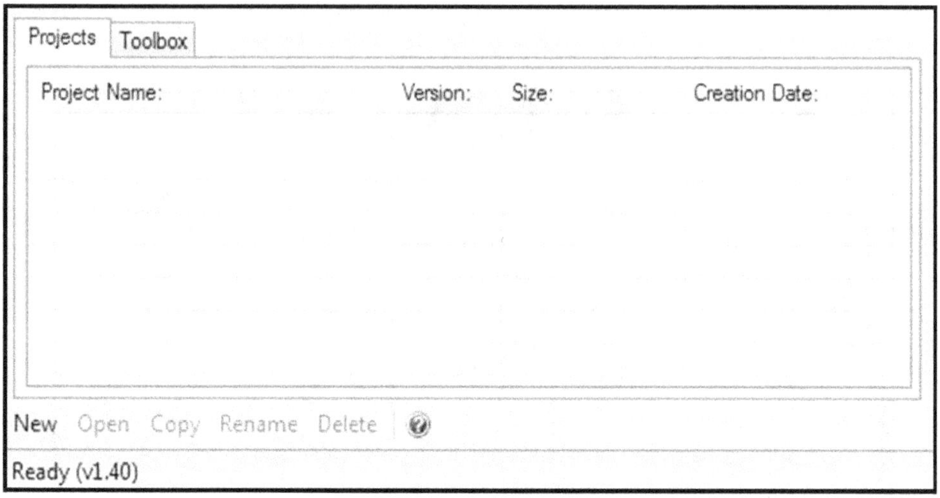

Figure 1.2 Project Manager Projects Tab

The projects tab contains the tools required to create new projects, as well as to copy, rename, and delete old projects.

Be sure to backup your projects on a regular basis.

The default location for Project Files is:
C:\Program Files (x86)\Solstar Games\Realm Crafter 1\Projects\<projectName>

New – Create a New Project
Choose New to create a fresh blank project. Please note that the project is not blank, but contains about 80 MB worth of files required to be "place holder" files for the Game Engine. This includes a basic set of scripts, actor models, and textures. You will probably want to go through the Master Media List in the Game Editor and delete all the files you are not using, as well as customize the file holder hierarchy to match your filing style. For now, leave all the files as they are; 80 MB is not that much space.

The default Project Name is "New Project".

Copy – Copy a Project
Select the project you wish to copy, and then click the Copy button to create the copy. The copied project will have "Copy of" at the beginning of its new Project Name.

Chapter 1: RCS Project Manager

There are times when you want to make a new version of an existing project. This is a good way to keep projects backed up. Every time you have a known good, working version, you can make a copy of the project files and increase the version number of your project.

For example, let's say you created a project called "Temple of Fear v1" and you add a new zone or a bunch of new weapons. You could save a copy of the project as "Temple of Fear v2". This way, if there ended up being a problem with v2, you could always go back to v1; the last known good copy.

Remember to copy a working project and make modifications to the copy, *not* the original.

Rename – Rename a Project
When you want to rename a project, use the Rename button.

Delete – Delete a Project
Sometimes you just want to wipe out the project and start over. Use the Delete function to destroy an existing project.

Toolbox Tab

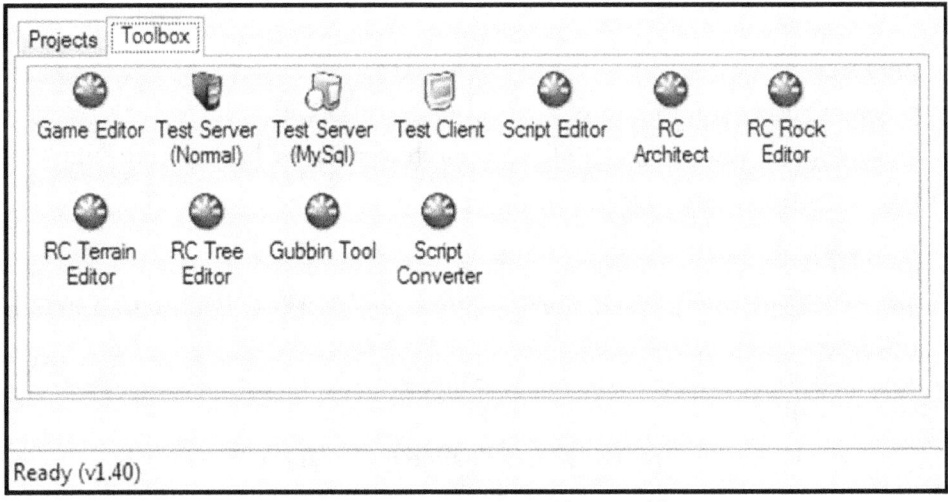

Figure 1.3 Project Manager Toolbox Tab

Game Editor
This is where you build your MMORPG. This program allows you to create a repository for media as well as define character attributes, damage types, and in-

Chapter 1: RCS Project Manager

game areas. The RCS Game Editor contains all the sub-editors required to create all aspects of your game. This is where you will do the bulk of the work required to bring your game idea to life.

Test Server (Normal)
If you want to test your game, you must run a Test Server and a Test Client. Be sure to unlock the Test Server before you attempt to connect any Test Clients.

Test Server (MySQL)
If you want your Test Server to have access to a MySQL database, you must run the Test Server MySQL version of the Test Server. This will allow the server to tie into the MySQL database system.

Test Client
Use the Test Client, along with the Text Server, to try out your game. This allows you to develop and test on the same computer, and to preview changes you've made.

Script Editor
The key to customizing your game is the use of scripting. Realm Crafter contains a basic script editor that is suitable for creating and editing game scripts. The editor includes a command reference.

RC Architect
This program allows you to create complex dungeons, castles, crypts, and other types of interiors. Areas created in the RC Architect can be brought into the RC Game Editor.

RC Rock Editor
This program helps you to create rocks and boulders that you can use to decorate the landscape.

RC Terrain Editor
The RC Terrain editor is a powerful and flexible tool you can use to make landscapes and populate them with buildings, trees, and more.

RC Tree Editor
The RC Tree program helps you make low polygon trees for RC that sway in the wind and change the colors of their leaves as the seasons change.

RC Gubbin Tool

This tool allows you to associate 3D meshes with Actor bones. Use this to line up where armor, weapons, and other accessories will be mounted when equipped in the game.

Script Converter

This tool converts old RC Script files to RC BVM scripts.

Chapter 2: RCS Game Editor

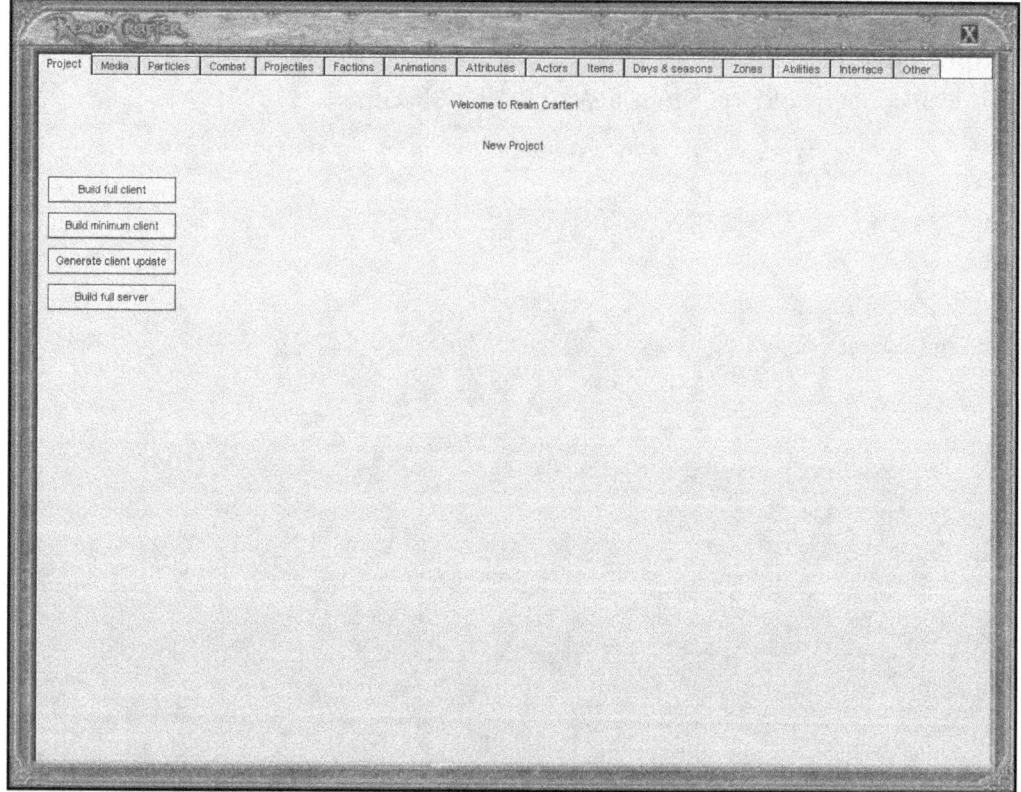

Figure 2.1 Game Editor

The Game Editor (GE) is where all the parts of your MMORPG project come together. Use the GE to bring your virtual world to life. Create areas in your world, decorate them with props and scenery, populate them with monsters and interesting NPC's, hide clever traps for unsuspecting travelers, set the weather conditions, and reward your players with treasure and valuable items.

The GE allows you to import 3D models, music, and other media from various sources and arrange them into a working project.

The media you import is mostly created outside of RCS with third-party software and brought into the Game Editor through the RCS Media Library.

Realm Crafter is not an MMORPG maker based on a certain type of game and rules system; it is an MMORPG Engine that you use to customize your own game. You supply all the parts of an MMORPG and use Realm Crafter to bring those parts together into a persistent, playable, virtual game world of your own design.

Because of the modular design of the GE, you can work on any part in any order you like. When it comes to being creative, everybody has a different style. Some like to lay out the landscape then add buildings and scenery. This is probably the most popular way, but if you prefer to create items first, you can certainly do it that way too. Find a way that works naturally and makes sense to you.

The Game Editor contains sections for all the common tools required to create an MMORPG. The editor lays these out as tabs.

The sections are as follows:

The Project Tab- This is where the Game Client and Game Server are created, using information programmed in the other Tabs.

The Media Tab- All media in the game must be present in the Media Database. Use this Tab to integrate 3D meshes, audio effects, and music into the game.

The Particles Tab- Rain, butterflies, waterfalls, falling leaves, snow, fire, smoke, and more can be simulated with Particles. Good use of particles adds environmental ambiance to your game.

The Combat Tab- Define the Damage Types, Combat Rules, and other Combat Properties on this Tab.

The Projectiles Tab- Does your game involve shooting things? Use this Tab to setup everything from fireballs to sling stones and arrows.

The Factions Tab- Friends and foes are important in MMORPG's. Use this Tab to define the significant social or political groups in your game; from warring clans of cave dwellers to space rebels and evil galactic empires, to giant mega-corporations and secret subversive societies.

The Animations Tab- Every animated 3D mesh can have animation sets that can be named and played. Use this Tab to define and name mesh animations.

The Attributes Tab- How strong are your characters? How smart? How quick? Attributes are a way to define the characteristics that define your characters. This

Chapter 2: Game Editor

Tab allows you to create those things that describe the physical and mental aspect of characters in your game.

The Actors Tab- Every "living" thing in the game is an Actor. Actors have Attributes, but most importantly, they have a Life attribute. The Player Characters, Vendors, and enemies are Actors. Likewise, so are the cows and chickens on the farm, and the alien drones and space frigates are Actors as well. Use this Tab to setup all the Actors in your game.

The Items Tab- Swords, potions, maps, laser guns, rings, gems, shields; all kinds of things players can use to help them through the game. Items represent the things you find along the way- things that you can store in your backpack, use, or wear. Use this Tab to define all the Items in your game.

The Days & Seasons Tab- Is your world very much like Earth in terms of seasons and days of the week? Alternatively, is your world an alien planet with 15-month years and 5-day weeks? Use this Tab to define your game's Calendar; from how many days in a week to when spring, summer, fall, and winter start and end. You can even invent new seasons.

The Zones Tab- Your MMORPG world is made up of collections of Zones, which represent locations for your players to explore. These locations can be as small as a jail cell to as large as a cave complex or even a large city. Use this Tab to define the Zones in your game.

The Abilities Tab- Roaming the world is nice, but being able to do things in the world is even better. Use Abilities to define special ways the players can interact with their world. Abilities simulate everything from combat maneuvers like Berserk Rage and Find Weakness to magic spells like Lightning and Fireball, or even sci-fi themed Abilities, such as Death Ray or Personal Shields. This Tab allows you to define all the different abilities possible in your game.

The Interface Tab- Use this Tab to layout the interface of your game. Place Attribute meters, status bars, and other indicators anywhere on the screen.

The Other Tab- Use this Tab to define the money system, and other miscellaneous properties not covered under other topic areas.

This comprehensive set of tools is detailed in the chapters that follow. Combining these tools in different ways gives you the flexibility to design whatever type of game you can imagine.

Chapter 3: Project Tab

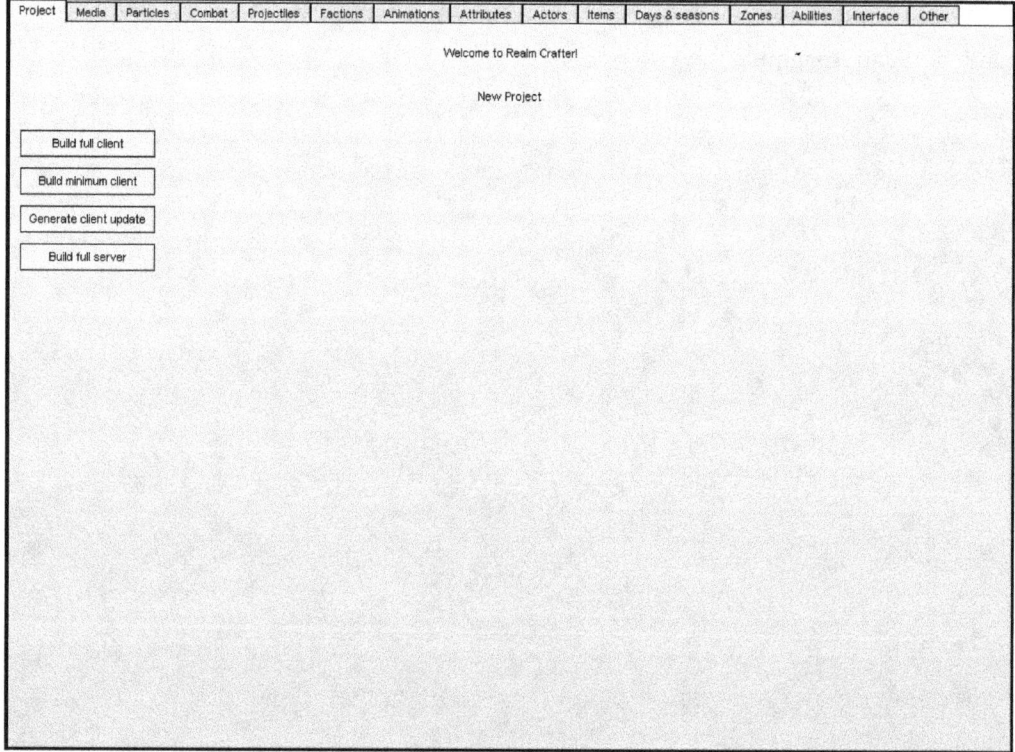

Figure 3.1 Project Tab

Project Tab Details

The Project Tab is where to go to build your project into matching Server and Client components, as well as for building game updates.

When the Full Client is built, it can be moved onto any compatible computer and run. You can package up the files in a ZIP archive or software installer and distribute the client program. All a user has to do is copy, unpack, or install the client and run the Game.exe program to launch the Game Client.

When the Full Server is built, it can be moved onto an appropriate server computer. Make sure the IP address on that computer matches the IP address you set in the Game Editor before you built the Game Client.

Build Full Client

Building a full client creates a new folder called "Game" located inside your project folder at:
\Realm Crafter 1\Projects\<project_name>\Game.

The Game Client can be launched by running Game.exe from inside the Game folder.

Generate Client Update

This generates a Game Client Update, as well as a Full Game Client and includes all the files needed by the Game Client in order to function. Use updates to keep Game Clients synchronized with your Game Content.

The update files get stored in a folder called "Files" inside a folder called "Patches", located inside the project folder at:
\Realm Crafter 1\Projects\<project_name>\Patches\Files.

Copy the files from the "Files" folder to your update web server. Overwrite existing updates with newer files; leave unchanged files if you want to save upload time.

It is a good idea to use different servers on different IP subnets. For instance, you may run the game server from your home on one Internet connection, and your update server from your home on a second internet connection.

The reason for using 2 different connections is that if you were to serve the updates from the same internet connection the game is being played on, you may suffer severe game play issues when un-patched clients log on and the bandwidth is used to serve them the patches.

There may be ways to setup QoS (Quality of Service) on certain routers to keep the Update Server from using too much bandwidth, giving preferential bandwidth to the game server, for instance, but that is beyond the scope of the RCS User's Manual.

Build Full Server

This option generates the Game Server part of the game. The server runs scripts and coordinates communications and movement between attached Clients. When you are ready to deploy your Server, click this button to generate a new copy of the Game Server.

The Server is built and placed in the "Server" folder located inside the project folder at:
\Realm Crafter 1\Projects\<project_name>\Server.

You can copy the Server folder to whatever computer you choose to act as the Game Server. Activate the Server program inside the Server folder to start the Game Server.

Be sure there is no firewall blocking the default port (25000) or any custom port you defined in the Other Tab in the Game Editor.

Chapter 4: Media Tab

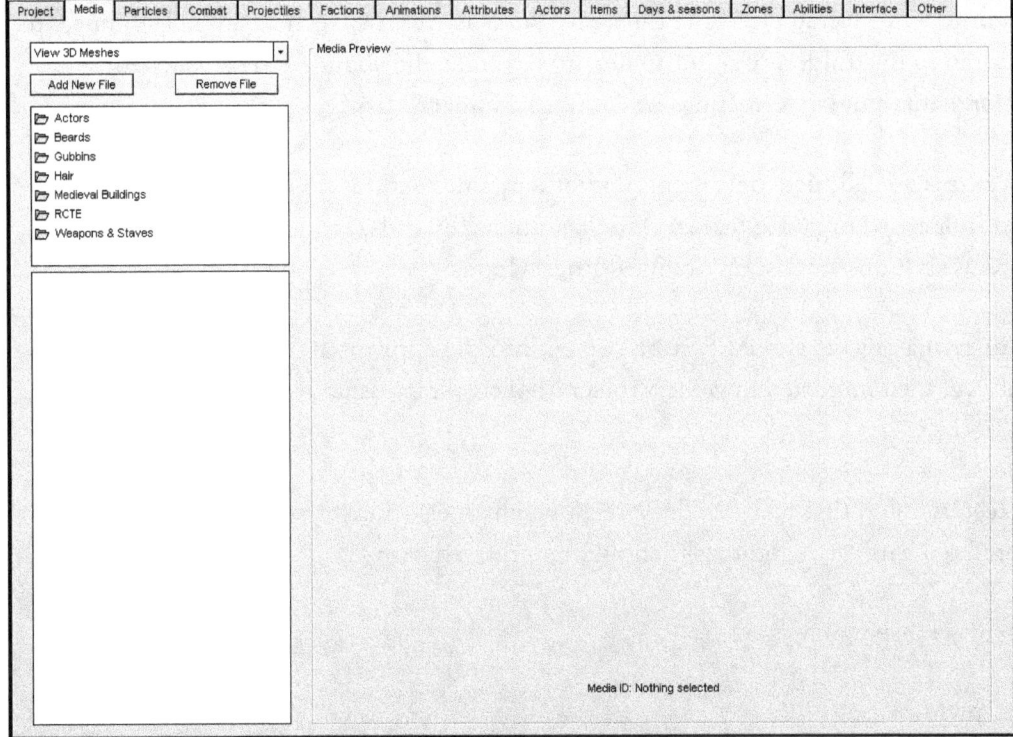

Figure 4.1 Media Tab

Media Tab Details

The Media Tab allows you to add and remove media, such as music, textures, 3D models, etc., to and from the Project Media Library.

Only objects brought into the Project Media Library can be used by the Project.

There are four special folders listed under:
\Realm Crafter 1\Projects\<project_name>\Game\Data

Meshes – All 3D objects in the game are filed under "Meshes". Use subfolders to organize the types of meshes, such as Actors\Human\Male, or Weapons\Swords\Shortswords.

Chapter 4: Media Tab

Music – All music for the game is stored in this folder. Use subfolders to organize the types of music, such as Combat\Orc, or Ambient\Forest, or Loading Screens\The Docks.

Sound – All sound effects in the game, such as Actor speech or animal sounds, are stored in this folder. Use subfolders to organize the sounds effects, such as Merchant\Human\Greetings or Combat\Human\Miss.

Textures – All the icons, maps, and other game textures go in this folder. Use subfolders to organize textures, such as Items/Swords/Icons or Items\Potions\Icons, or Abilities\Priest\Icons.

All media objects should first be copied into the appropriate folders mentioned above, then imported into the Project Media Library using the Media Tab of the RCS GE.

Keep in mind that textures that are alpha channels (transparency map) should be prefixed with "a_" and masks should be prefixed with "m_". For example:

a_myTransparancy.png

m_myMask.png

Use alpha to make semitransparent areas. A grayscale alpha channel controls alpha levels; white is not transparent, black is 100% transparent, gray is 50% transparent. Use this to control opacity of glass or ice.

Use masks to make black areas transparent. For instance, the area between the wire in a chain-link fence; it's completely clear – you can see right through.

Media Library View Selection List

Use the View Selection List to designate what type of media you want to import or preview.

View 3D Meshes

This list contains all the 3D game assets and allows you to preview, add, or delete 3D media objects from the Project Media Library.

Chapter 4: Media Tab

View Textures
This list contains all the Texture game assets and allows you to preview, add, or delete texture media objects from the Project Media Library.

View Sounds
This list contains all the sound effect game assets and allows you to preview, add, or delete sound effect media objects from the Project Media Library.

View Music
This list contains all the Music game assets and allows you to preview, add, or delete music media objects from the Project Media Library.

Add New File
Adding a new file to the texture library brings up a file dialog, where you can choose the media file you want to bring in, as well as some options on how to import the media.

Adding 3D Meshes
Meshes are 3D models that can be imported and used as scenery or actors. Create 3D meshes in any common 3D modeling program, such as Blender.

3D File Formats Supported
Realm Crafter can use a few different 3D mesh formats.

- **.b3d** – Blitz 3D format. This is the required format for animated meshes.
- **.eb3d** – Encrypted Blitz 3D format.
- **.x** – Windows Direct X 3D format for models only; no animation.
- **.3ds** – 3D Studio format for models only; no animation.

3D Mesh Options
Mesh is Animated
Select this if the mesh contains an animation track. Currently only .b3d mesh animations are supported.

Encrypt Where Possible
Select this to convert .b3d into .eb3d format, effectively encrypting the mesh.

Chapter 4: Media Tab

Adding Textures

Please note: Any visual media that needs to duplicate extreme detail (such as player maps or notes or signs with writing or menus) should NOT use a lossy compression format, such as jpg or dds. Instead, consider using a lossless format, such as bmp, png, or tga.

Texture File Formats Supported

- **.bmp** – Microsoft bitmap format. This lossless format can be compressed and at 32 bits per pixel contains an alpha channel that holds transparency information.
- **.jpg** – Joint Photographic Experts Group format. This lossy format can be compressed. The amount of loss of detail is increased as the file size is decreased. Therefore, a balance between detail and compression must be achieved for acceptable results. Also, note that jpeg format does not include an alpha channel to control transparency.
- **.png** – Portable Network Graphics format. This lossless format can be compressed. This format also contains an alpha channel to control transparency.
- **.tga** – Truevision Targa format. This lossless format can also be compressed. This format also contains an alpha channel to control transparency. This compression format is best used on images with large areas of similar colors. The compression does not work as good with high detail, such as photographs.
- **.dds** – Microsoft Direct Draw Surface format. This lossy format can be compressed into a form that is quickly decompressed using graphics cards with modern Graphics Processing Units. This format is a component of Microsoft's DirectX architecture.

Texture Options

When importing textures, it is important to tell the GE how you intend to use the texture. You may choose multiple attributes by checking multiple boxes that apply.

Color

Select this if the texture is in color. If it is a grayscale texture, such as a height map, leave this unchecked.

Alpha

Select this if the texture contains an alpha channel. Alpha channels contain a grayscale overlay that dictates the relative transparency of various parts of the texture.

Black is 100% transparent, white is 100% opaque, gray is 50% transparent.

Masked
Select this if the texture is to be masked.

Black pixels would be 100% transparent. There is no option for semi-transparency.

If you wish to have black pixels that are not transparent, use RGB 0, 0, 1 to simulate black. It is dark enough blue to be indiscernible from black.

Mipmapped
Mipmapped textures contain a set of lower resolution textures that are used when rendering objects at certain distances from the camera, in effect providing a Level of Detail for the texture, saving the renderer from calculating textures at a distance.

If your texture is .dds format, it should already include mipmapping.

*Note: Do not use mipmapped on anything that has writing. Mipmapping writing makes it blurry and sometimes unreadable.

Clamp U
This option is used for textures that will be applied to 3D objects. If checked, it prevents the texture from repeating on the horizontal axis.

Clamp V
This option is used for textures that will be applied to 3D objects. If checked, it prevents the texture from repeating on the vertical axis.

Sphere Map
Select this option if the texture is a sphere map. Sphere maps are used for things such as sky, clouds, and stars.

Cube Map
Select this option if the texture is a cube map. Cube maps are used for sky boxes or simple reflection maps.

Chapter 4: Media Tab

Adding Sounds

When adding sounds, you are given the option to make the sound 3D. Making a sound 3D means that the sound volume will diminish as the actor moves from the center of the sound zone.

Leaving the 3D option unchecked means to play the sound evenly across the sound zone.

Sound / Audio Formats Supported

- **.wav** – Microsoft Waveform format. This audio format can be compressed or uncompressed. It is most commonly used in its uncompressed format.
- **.raw** – RAW audio format. This audio format is uncompressed.
- **.mp3** – Moving Pictures Experts Group audio format. This format can be compressed and uses a lossy algorithm.
- **.ogg** – OGG audio format. This audio format can be compressed with lossy or lossless codecs.

Adding Music

Theme music for different areas can be nice, but don't overdo it. Remember that instead of music looping, you could use another kind of special effect sound, like rain or crickets.

Music Formats Supported

- **.mp3** – Moving Pictures Experts Group audio format. This format can be compressed and uses a lossy algorithm.
- **.ogg** – OGG audio format. This audio format can be compressed with lossy or lossless codecs.
- **.mid** – Musical Instrument Digital Interface format. This format does not store audio waveforms, but it does allow sequencing of notes using a computer's on-board sound card for instrument sources.
- **.wav** – Microsoft Waveform format. This audio format can be compressed or uncompressed. It is most commonly used in its uncompressed format.
- **.mod** – MOD audio format. This is a file format widely used by Amiga computers, but has had continued support in many forms since the Amiga was discontinued. This format is similar to MIDI, but contains the instrument waveforms. It is commonly used for background music.
- **.s3m** – SM3 Audio format is an extension of the MOD format, allowing more channels and more instruments.
- **.xm** – Extended Module audio format.
- **.it** – Impulse tracker is a multi-track digital music sequencer for DOS.

Remove File

If you are no longer going to use a media object, it is a good idea to remove it from your project AND from the hard drive. You have the option of doing both under this button.

Folder Navigator

Use this area to navigate between folders in order to find and select the media you wish to preview.

Use a good organization of category hierarchies to help keep your media organized.

File Selector

Use the File Selector to select the individual file you wish to preview in the Media Preview Window.

Media Preview Window

This window shows a preview of the object currently selected in the File Selector box.

Media ID

Media ID is used to identify specific pieces of media in the Project Media Library.

Initial Scale (In 3D Mesh Selection only)

Set the initial object scale with this controller. Sometimes 3D models from various sources will come into the project at too high or too low a scale. Use this control to set the initial size of the 3D mesh you are importing.

Chapter 5: Particles Tab

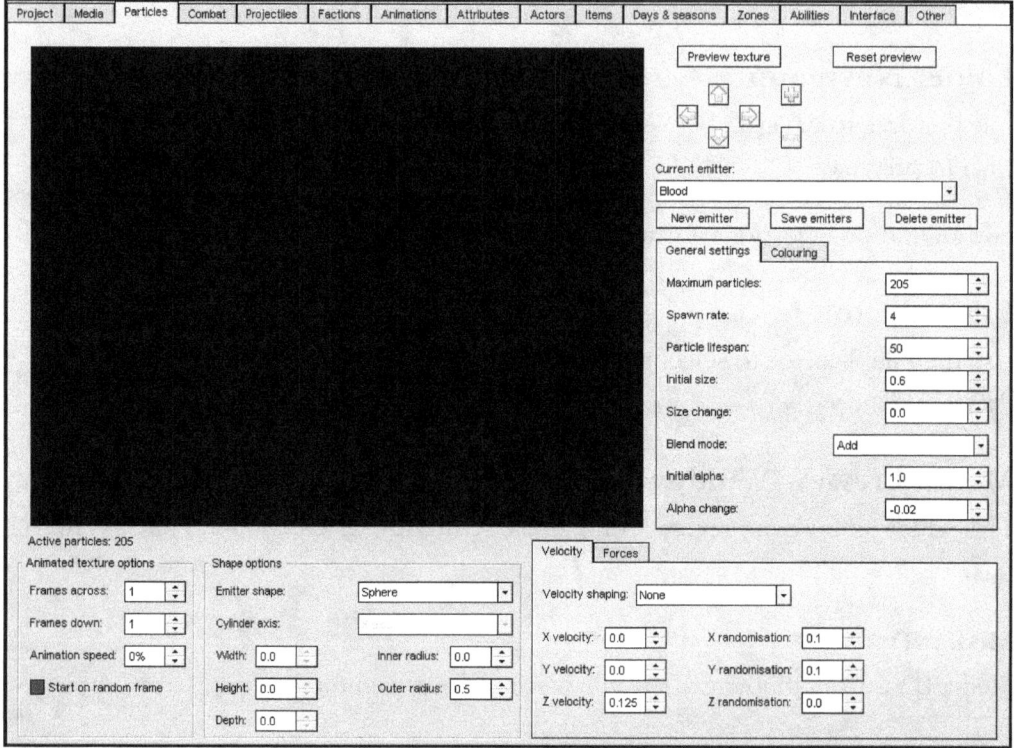

Figure 5.1 Particles Tab

Particles Tab Details

Particles can be used for anything from fire and smoke to rain and snow. Swarms of bugs, falling leaves, all these things and more can be simulated with clever use of the particle system.

Particle Preview Window

This window displays a preview of the currently selected particle in action.

Active Particles

This readout displays the current number of active particles displayed in the Preview Window.

Preview Texture

This button allows you to change the texture used for the particles.

Reset Preview

Sometimes the changes you make to the settings are not always reflected properly in the Preview Window; sometimes you might get the preview window in a disoriented position. Using the Reset Preview button puts the preview back in the center of the Preview Window, reflecting the current particle setting correctly.

Preview Adjustment Controls

Arrows

The arrows are used to rotate the camera around the texture so you can look at it from multiple angles.

Up Arrow:	Rotate camera up.
Down Arrow:	Rotate camera down.
Left Arrow:	Rotate the camera to the left.
Right Arrow:	Rotate the camera to the right.
+/- (plus and minus):	The plus and minus signs are used to zoom in and zoom out respectively.

Current Emitter Selection List

This drop-down list is used to select a particle from the existing list. All the particle's settings will be loaded into the respective fields for review or editing.

New Emitter

Use this control to create a fresh new emitter.

Save Emitters

The emitters are automatically saved when you exit the Game Editor, but remember to save frequently in case of a power outage or other catastrophe. Use this button to save the current emitter list and settings.

Delete Emitter

Use this control to erase particles from the Particle List. Deleted particles cannot be restored, so only use this if you are sure you want the currently selected particle to disappear forever.

Chapter 5: Particles Tab

General Settings Tab

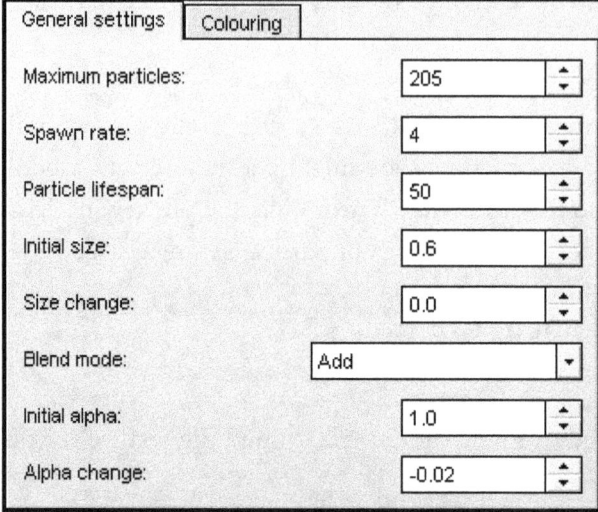

Figure 5.2 Particle General Settings Tab

Maximum Particles

This sets the maximum number of particles that can be held in the Particle Pool at one time.

Spawn Rate

This sets how many particles are spawned from the Particle Pool per frame.

Particle Lifespan

This sets how long each particle lasts in frames before it is destroyed and sent back to the Particle Pool.

Initial Size

This is the starting size of the particle. This number can be set to a fraction, so if you want the particle to start at half of its original size, then set the control to 0.5.

The lower the number, the smaller the starting size, the larger the number, that larger the starting particle size.

Size Change

If you want to change the size of the particle over its lifespan, you can enter a value here. The larger the value, the more the particle will grow over its lifespan. The lower the value, the more the particle will shrink over its lifespan.

For instance, if you want the particle to increase in size by 10% per frame, use a setting of 0.1, if you want the particle to decrease in size by 10% per frame, use a setting of -0.1.

Blend Mode

The normal setting for Blend Mode is Add.

- **Normal**- The particle is drawn without any blending. Each particle looks like the bitmap it is made of, complete with borders.
- **Multiply**- Pixel values are multiplied when they overlap each other. Pixel values become darker when they overlay each other, or a dark background. Masks become opaque. This creates the opposite effect as Add.
- **Add**- Pixels values are added when they overlay each other. This creates a brighter effect when the particles stack on top of each other. The texture map also has its mask applied as transparent, so no borders are seen.

Initial Alpha

Alpha determines how transparent the particle is. A setting of one means the particle starts opaque. A starting setting of 0.5 means the particle starts semi-transparent.

Alpha Change

This sets the changes to the alpha levels over time. Set this to a negative number to make the particle more transparent over its lifespan. Set this to a positive number to make the particle more opaque over time.

For instance, if you want the particle to become 10% more transparent every frame, set this value to -0.1, if you want the particle to become 10% less transparent every frame of its lifespan, use a setting of 0.1.

Chapter 5: Particles Tab

Coloring Tab

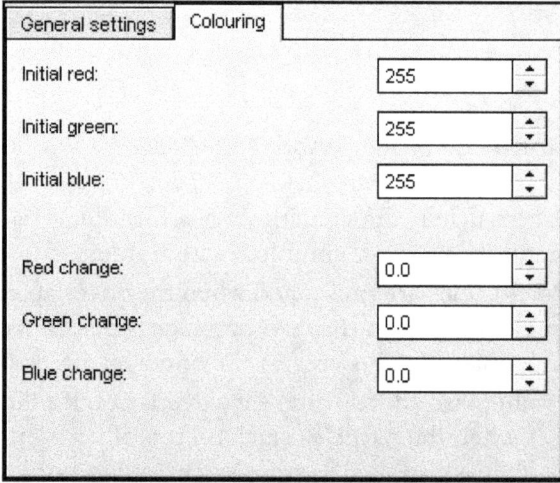

Figure 5.3 Particle Coloring Tab

This tab allows control of the color tinting of a particle over its lifespan. The initial setting for Red, Green, and Blue, are 255 each. This means the particle will be lit or tinted with white light (RGB value of 255, 255, 255 means white). If you want the particle to be lit with a dim white light then use a value like 100 or even 10. If you want the particle to be lit with a dark blue light, then set the RGB values to 0, 0, 255.

Color values range from 0 (no color in that channel) to 255 (maximum amount of that color channel).

Initial Red
Sets the initial Red value of the color tinting applied to a particle at the moment it is created.

Initial Green
Sets the initial Green value of the color tinting applied to a particle at the moment it is created.

Initial Blue
Sets the initial Blue value of the color tinting applied to a particle at the moment it is created.

Red Change
This is how much you want the Red level to change over the particle's lifespan.

Green Change

This is how much you want the Green level to change over the particle's lifespan.

Blue Change

This is how much you want the Blue level to change over the particle's lifespan.

Chapter 5: Particles Tab

Animated Texture Options

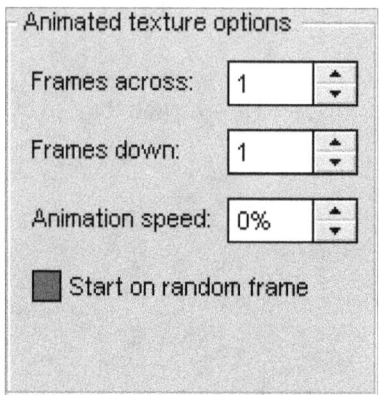

Figure 5.4 Animated Texture Options

You can create your own animated textures that are overlaid on the particle. To do this, you must provide an image strip with the frames of animation side by side. The size in pixels must be in powers of two. For instance, your strip could be two 16x16 frames set side by side for a 32x16 graphic.

Animations are looped repeatedly during the lifespan of the particle.

Frames Across
This sets how many frames across to divide the image strip. In our example of a 32x16 image strip, we would enter a value of 2 in this box, since the image is 2 frames long.

Frames Down
This is how many frames tall the image strip is. In our example of the 32x16 image strip, we would enter a value of 1, since the image strip is only 1 frame high.

Animation Speed
This sets how fast to playback the animation. Setting this at 0% means no animation. Setting this at 100% means to advance by 1 frame per frame. Setting this to 50% means to advance 1 frame every 2 frames. Setting this to 25% means to advance 1 frame every 4 frames, etc.

Start on Random Frame
Check this box if you want your animation to start on a random frame, instead of the first frame in the set.

Shape Options

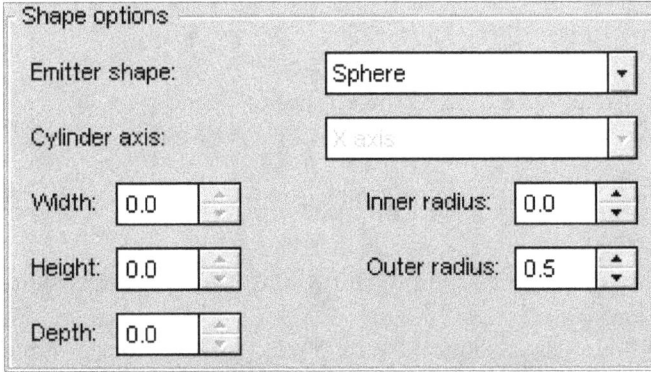

Figure 5.5 Particle Emitter Shape Options

This is where the shape of the emitter is defined. Different emitters allow different effects. Some examples might be using a sphere shape to make an explosion of stars, using a cylinder to spawn particles in a ring shape, or using a long narrow box emitter to spawn particles in the shape of a waterfall.

Emitter Shape List

Use this drop down list to select the type of emitter you want to use for your particle.

- **Sphere**- Use a sphere emitter to create a globe of particles. Particles spawn from random locations within the sphere. If you want your sphere to have a "hollow" center, adjust the inner radius so that it is larger than zero, but smaller than the Outer Radius setting.
- **Cylinder**- Use a cylinder emitter to create a column or ring of particles. Particles spawn from random locations within the cylinder.
- **Box**- Use a box emitter to create rectangular areas of particles. Particles spawn at a random location within the confines of a box.

Cylinder Axis List

This setting only applies when the Emitter Shape is set to Cylinder.

Width

This control sets the width of the Sphere, Cylinder, or Box (X axis).

Height

This sets the height of the Sphere, Cylinder, or Box (Y axis).

Chapter 5: Particles Tab

Depth
This sets the depth of the Sphere, Cylinder, or Box (Z axis).

Inner Radius
This control sets the inner radius of the sphere or cylinder.

Outer Radius
This control sets the outer radius of the sphere or cylinder.

X Axis- The cylinder axis is aligned to the X axis (the cylinder is sideways).

Y Axis- The cylinder axis is aligned to the Y axis (the cylinder is standing upright)

Z Axis- The cylinder axis is aligned with the Z axis (the cylinder is sideways, perpendicular to the X axis)

Chapter 5: Particles Tab

Velocity Tab

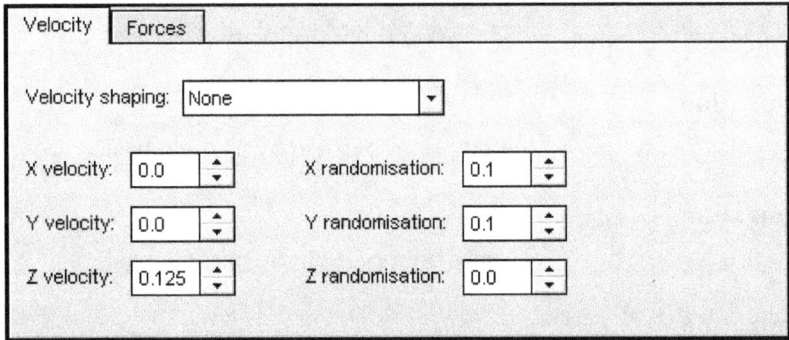

Figure 5.6 Particle Velocity Tab

Velocity sets the speed of movement of a particle on a given axis. Increase the velocity to "shoot" the particle out of the emitter at a high speed.

Velocity Shaping List

Velocity Shaping determines the pattern with which new particles are generated.

- **None**- Particles are spawned within the "bounding box" of the emitter and travel in a straight line according to the Velocity settings.
- **Shaped**- Particles are spawned within the "bounding box" of the emitter and travel in a straight line in both directions of the travelling axis according to the Velocity settings.
- **Strictly Shaped**- Particles are spawned within the "bounding box" of the emitter and travel in a straight line in both directions of the axis according to the Velocity settings. With this setting, about half the particles linger at their origin, while the other half behave as if set to Shaped. If the velocity in any single axis is greater than the velocity of the other two axes (compared individually), the particle will move along the stronger velocity's axes. For example, if VX > VY and VX > VZ, the particle will move on the X axis.

X Velocity

This is the horizontal velocity of the particle. If you want your particle to move right or left, increase or decrease the X Velocity.

Y Velocity

This is the vertical velocity of the particle. If you want your particle to rise over time, increase the Y Velocity. If you want your particle to fall, decrease the Y Velocity.

Chapter 5: Particles Tab

Z Velocity

This is the horizontal velocity of the particle. If you want your particle to move forward or backward, increase or decrease the Z Velocity.

X Randomization

This allows you to vary the X Velocity on a particle by particle basis.

Y Randomization

This allows you to vary the Y Velocity on a particle by particle basis.

Z Randomization

This allows you to vary the Z Velocity on a particle by particle basis.

Chapter 5: Particles Tab

Forces Tab

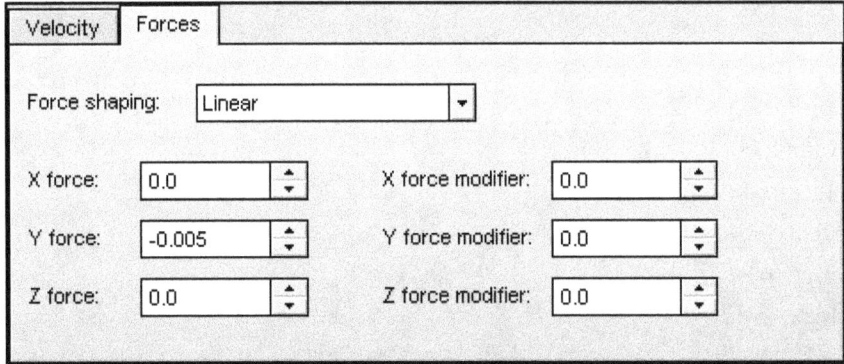

Figure 5.7 Particle Forces Tab

Forces act against the particle Velocity. Use Forces to simulate gravity, current, or wind.

Force Shaping List
- **Linear**- Force is applied in a line.
- **Spherical-** Force is applied on an angle.

X Force
The force applied to the particle on the X axis. Use this for simulating wind or currents.

Y Force
The force applied to the particle on the Y axis. Use this for simulating gravity.

Z Force
The force applied to the particle on the Z axis. Use this for simulating wind or currents.

X Force Modifier
This allows you to vary the X Force on a particle by particle basis.

Y Force Modifier
This allows you to vary the Y Force on a particle by particle basis.

Z Force Modifier
This allows you to vary the Z Force on a particle by particle basis.

Chapter 5: Particles Tab

Sample Particle

Sparks
General Settings
Maximum Particles: 20
Spawn Rate: 5
Particle Lifespan: 30
Initial Size: 0.01
Size Change: 0
Blend Mode: Add
Initial Alpha: 1
Alpha Change: -0.002

Coloring
Initial Red: 255
Initial Green: 255
Initial Blue: 153
Red Change: -15
Green Change: -25
Blue Change: -10

Shape Options
Emitter Shape: Box
Width: 0
Height: 0
Depth: 0
Velocity

Velocity Shaping: None
X Velocity: 0
Y Velocity: 0.1
Z Velocity: 0.0
X Randomization: 0.05
Y Randomization: 0
Z Randomization: 0.05

Forces
Force Shaping: Linear
X Force: 0
Y Force: -0.007
Z Force: 0
X Force Modifier: 0
Y Force Modifier: 0
Z Force Modifier: 0

Chapter 6: Combat Tab

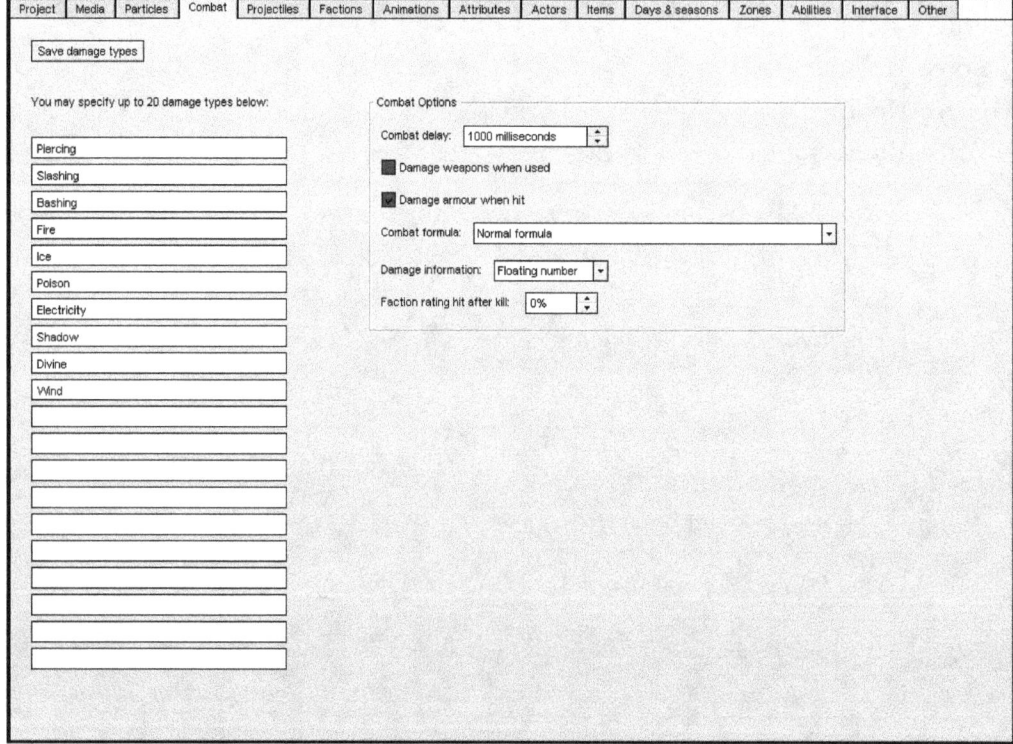

Figure 6.1 Combat Tab

Combat Tab Details
The Combat Tab is where Damage Types and other aspects of combat are defined.

Save Damage Types
This button saves the current Damage Types List.

List of Damage Types
You may specify up to 20 types of damage for your game. Damage types can vary from armor to armor and weapon to weapon.

Chapter 6: Combat Tab

Typical damage types include such things as:

- Crushing
- Slashing
- Piercing
- Acid
- Electricity
- Fire
- Cold
- Magic

Combat Options

Combat Delay
This sets how often the combat script is called during combat.

Damage Weapons When Used
This sets an option to damage weapons during combat so that weapons eventually wear out and need to be repaired or replaced.

This is used for the built-in combat script. If using a custom combat script, Damage to Weapon must be calculated and applied by the script.

Damage Armor When Hit
This option controls whether or armor is damaged by hits during combat so that armor eventually wears out and needs to be repaired or replaced.

This is used for the built-in combat script. If using a custom combat script, Armor Damage must be calculated and applied by the script.

Combat Formula: Built-In
The built-in combat formulas always do at least 1 point of damage.

The built-in combat formulas also run faster than the custom combat scripts, since they are programmed into the game engine directly.

Normal Formula
If unarmed or weapon is damaged below 1%, the Normal Formula is:
Damage = ((Strength / 8) + rand (-5, 5)) - (TotalArmor + (Toughness / 8))

Chapter 6: Combat Tab

If a weapon is equipped that is not damaged below 1%, and the attacker Strength is less than the weapon damage, the Normal Formula is:
Damage = (WeaponDamage - rand(5, 8)) - (TotalArmor + (Toughness / 8))

If a weapon is equipped that is not damaged below 1%, and the attacker Strength is greater than the weapon damage, the Normal Formula is:
Damage = (WeaponDamage + rand(5, 8)) - (TotalArmor + (Toughness / 8))

If a weapon is equipped that is not damaged below 1% and the attacker Strength is equal to the weapon damage, the Normal Formula is:
Damage = (WeaponDamage + rand (-5, 5)) - (TotalArmor + (Toughness / 8))

No Strength Bonus or Penalty
This formula is the same as the Normal Formula, but without a bonus or penalty for Strength.

If unarmed or weapon is damaged below 1%, the Normal Formula is:
Damage = ((Strength / 8) + rand (-5, 5)) - (TotalArmor + (Toughness / 8))

If a weapon is equipped that is not damaged below 1%, the Normal Formula is:
Damage = WeaponDamage - (TotalArmor + (Toughness / 8))

High Damage, High Defense
In this formula the Strength bonus, TotalArmor, and Toughness are exaggerated. Armor is multiplied by toughness.

If unarmed or weapon is not damaged below 1%, the Normal Formula is:
Damage = (Strength + rand (-10, 10)) - (TotalArmor * Toughness))

If a weapon is equipped that is not damaged below 1%, the Normal Formula is:
Damage = (WeaponDamage * Strength) - (TotalArmor * Toughness)

Use the Attack Script
This option sets the Game Server to use the Custom Attack Script.

Animations, damage, chances to hit, dodge, defend, etc. must all be programmed by hand if using a Custom Attack Script.

Use the Attack.rsl script to hold your Custom Attack Script, or edit the source code if you have access to it.

Chapter 6: Combat Tab

Damage Information

This option selects how combat damage is displayed to the user.

- **None** – No damage information is conveyed to the user.
- **Chat Message** – Damage information is displayed in the Chat Window.
- **Floating Number** – Damage information is displayed as a floating number in the main display window.

Faction Rating Hit After Kill

This sets how much the victim's Faction Rating will change when the victim is killed. Faction value helps members of that faction decide if you are a friend (positive faction rating) or an enemy (negative faction rating). Faction rating can also be changed through scripting for such things as in-game deeds, completing faction quests, etc.

Chapter 7: Projectiles Tab

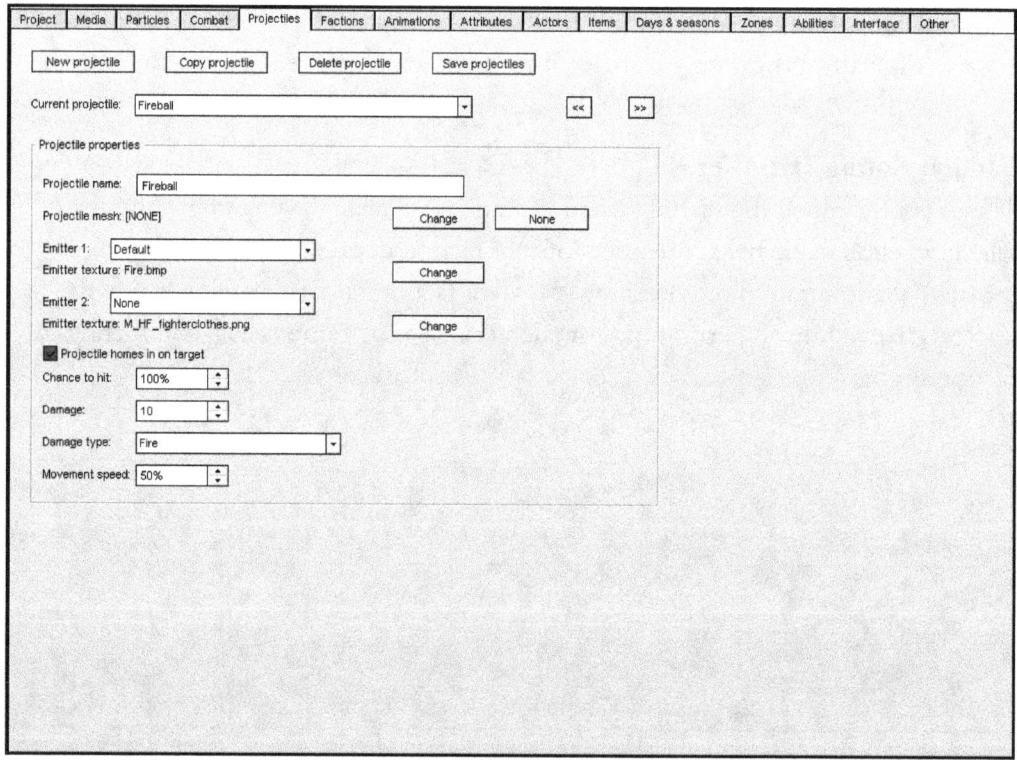

Figure 7.1 Projectiles Tab

Projectiles Tab Details

The Projectiles Tab is where things such as spells, arrows, throwing knives, etc. are defined.

Projectiles are activated through scripting.

Managing the Projectiles List

The Game Editor gives us several options for creating, deleting, navigating, and managing the Projectiles List.

New Projectile

This button creates a new entry in the Projectile List.

Chapter 7: Projectiles Tab

Copy Projectile
This button copies the currently selected projectile and creates a new entry in the Projectile List.

Delete Projectile
This button removes the currently selected projectile from the Projectile List.

Save Projectiles
This button saves the Projectile List.

Current Projectile
This shows the currently selected projectile.

Projectile Selection Controls
Different projectiles can be selected from the Projectile List using these controls. All the remaining fields on this page depend on what is selected in this field. Use the drop-down list, and arrow buttons to select the Current Projectile you wish to edit or review.

Projectile Properties
These properties define the various features of the currently selected Projectile.

Projectile Name
Use this control to change the name of the projectile.

Projectile Mesh
This displays the 3D mesh associated with the projectile.

Change
Use this control to select the 3D mesh you want to use for the projectile. The mesh must be previously loaded into the Master Media List.

None
Use this control to set the 3D mesh for the projectile to NONE if there is no associated mesh (i.e. - for invisible spell effects).

Emitter 1 List
Use this control to choose one of the particle emitters that you have already defined under the Particles Tab.

Chapter 7: Projectiles Tab

Emitter 1 Texture
Use this to set the texture for the emitter indicated in Emitter 1 List control (see above).

Change
Use this control to change the texture used in Emitter 1.

Emitter 2 List
Use this control to choose one of the particle emitters that you have already defined under the Particles Tab.

Emitter 2 Texture
Use this to set the texture for the emitter indicated in Emitter 2 List control (see above).

Change
Use this control to change the texture used in Emitter 2.

Projectile Homes in on Target Option
Use this option to set whether or not the projectile homes in on its target.

Chance to Hit
This is the percentage chance the projectile will hit its target.

Damage
This controls how much damage the projectile does when it hits.

Damage Type
This is the type of damage the projectile does when it hits. Damage types are taken from the Combat Tab.

Movement Speed
This determines how fast the projectile travels to its target.

Chapter 8: Factions Tab

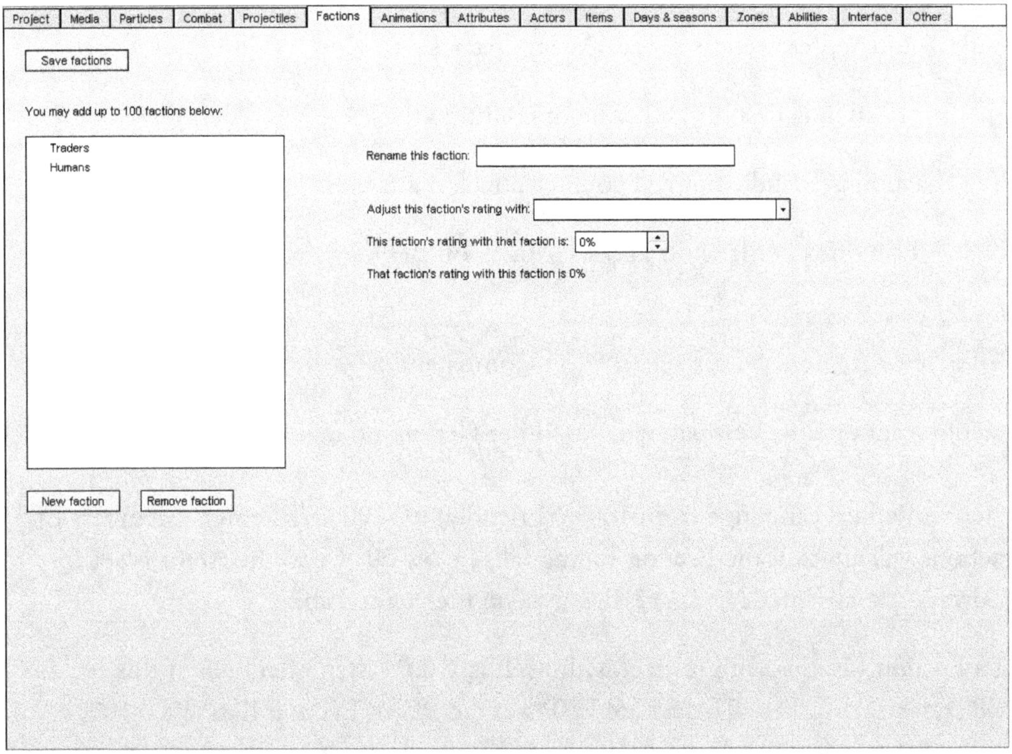

Figure 8.1 Factions Tab

Factions Tab Details

Factions are a way to measure an Actor's standing with regards to members of other groups.

You may create up to 100 factions.

The most basic factions might be "Player", "NPC", "Animal", and "Monster", but there are many more possibilities, such as "Merchants", "Wild Animals", "Pirates", "Humans", "Dwarves", "Elves", "Town Guards", etc.

With Actor Aggressiveness set at "Passive":

The Faction is passive and will never counter-attack no matter the Faction Rating.

With Actor Aggressiveness set at "Defensive":

Chapter 8: Factions Tab

51% + : Faction is friendly and will not counter-attack.

50% - : Faction is friendly but will counter-attack if attacked.

With Actor Aggressiveness set at "Always Attacks":

51% + : Faction is friendly and will not counter-attack.

50% :Faction is friendly but will counter-attack if attacked.

49% - : Faction is not friendly and will attack on sight.

With Actor Aggressiveness set at "Non-Combatant":

Faction cannot enter combat with any other faction, no matter the Faction Rating.

Faction Ratings can range from 100% (Friendly) to -100% (Enemy). Members of factions will attack if the Faction Rating falls below 50%, and the Actor is set for "Always Attacks" under "Aggressiveness" in the Actor Tab.

If a Faction's Rating with respect with itself is -100% then members of this faction will attack each-other. To activate PVP, set the Player Faction Rating to -100% with respect to itself and turn on PvP for the particular Zone (see the section on Zone Tab).

It can be very useful to create your own faction relationship chart.

Example of a basic Faction relationship chart might look like this:

	Player	NPC	Animal	Monster
Player	100% (Players do not attach other players)	100% (Players do not attack NPC's)	-100% (Players can attack animals)	-100% (Players can attack monsters)
NPC	100% (NPC's do not attack players NPC's)	100% (NPC's do not attack other NPC's)	100% (NPC's do not attack Animals)	-100% (NPC's can attack Monsters)
Animal	100% (Animals do not attack Players)	100% (Animals do not attack NPC's)	100% (Animals do not attack other Animals)	100% (Animals do not attack Monsters)
Monster	-100% (Monsters always attack Players)	-100% (Monsters always attack NPC)	-100% (Monsters always attack Animals)	100% (Monsters do not attack other Monsters)

Figure 8.2 Faction Relationship Chart

Managing the Factions List

This section of the Factions Tab contains controls for creating, deleting, and managing the Factions List.

Factions List

This box lists all the Factions in the game and lets you select one to modify.

New Faction

Use this button to create a new Faction.

After the new Faction is created, set the Faction Rating with respect to the other Factions using the "Adjust This Faction's Rating With" control.

Remove Faction

This button deletes a Faction from the Faction List.

Chapter 8: Factions Tab

Rename This Faction

Use this control to change the name of the currently selected Faction.

Adjusting Faction Ratings

This area is where ratings are set with respect to other Factions.

Adjust This Faction's Rating With

Use this control to select a Faction and set its rating with respect to the currently selected Faction.

This Faction's Rating With That Faction Is

Enter the Faction Rating with respect to the Faction chosen in "Adjust This Faction's Rating With", above.

Reciprocal Faction Rate Readout

This displays the current Faction rating from the point of view of the Enter the Faction Rating with respect to the Faction chosen in "Adjust This Faction's Rating With", above.

Chapter 9: Animations Tab

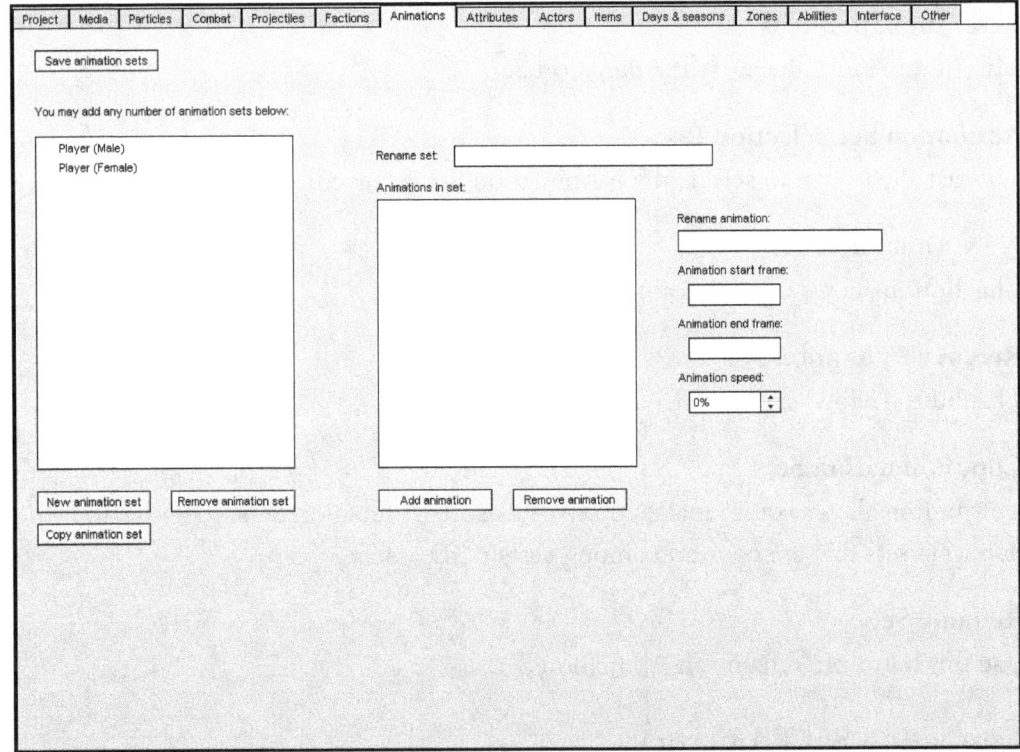

Figure 9.1 Animations Tab

Animations Tab Details

The Animations Tab is where Animation Sets are defined for various in-game Actors and animated scenery. This is done by defining ranges of frames that correspond to the various animations that are contained within the .b3d file. When you define animations for your 3D objects, you must record which frames each animation starts and ends on and transfer that information into the various fields in the Animation Tab.

For example, if you have a wolf Actor, you might have an Animation Set that contains animations for Run (frames 1-30), Sit (frames 31-44), Bite (frames 44-69), etc.

** Note: The RC Game Client will only allow animations on .b3d (or .eb3d) files.

Chapter 9: Animations Tab

Managing Animation Sets
This area contains all the controls needed to create, delete, and manage Animation Sets.

Save Animation Sets
This button saves the current Animation Set.

Animation Set Selection List
This list allows you to select which Animation Set is currently being edited.

New Animation Set
This button allows you to create a new Animation Set.

Remove Animation Set
This button allows you to delete an Animation Set.

Copy Animation Set
This button allows you to make copies of existing Animation Sets. Use this to duplicate sets that are common among certain 3D assets.

Rename Set
Use this button to rename an Animation Set.

Animation Set Properties
This area contains controls for the Animation Set details.

Animations in Set Selection List
Each Animation set can have a selection of Animations within it. For instance, you may have an Animation Set called "Human Fighter" that contains Animations for walk, run, jump, swim, stab, dodge, parry, dance, etc. These individual Animations are contained within the Animation Set.

Add Animation
Use this button to create a new Animation within the currently selected Animation Set.

Remove Animation
Use this button to remove Animations from the currently selected Animation Set.

Rename Animation
Use this button to rename Animations in the currently selected Animation Set.

Animation Start Frame

Use this field to indicate the starting frame of the current Animation within the selected Animation Set.

Animation End Frame

Use this field to indicate the ending frame of the current Animation within the selected Animation Set.

Animation Speed

Use this spinner to indicate how fast you want the current Animation to play back when triggered. This value can also be set from scripting.

Chapter 10: Attributes Tab

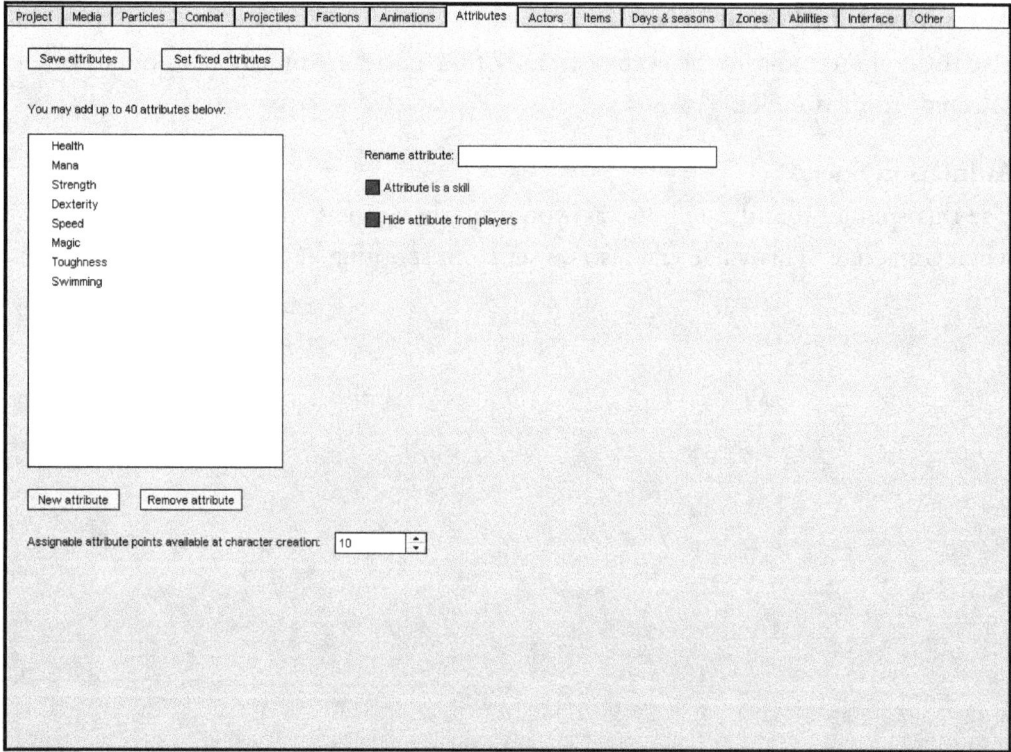

Figure 10.1 Attributes Tab

Attributes Tab Details

Attributes are the core of most Role Playing Games; the give relative values to a Player's characteristics. They typically have a maximum and current value. For instance, a character might have a maximum health of 100 when she is undamaged, but might currently be at only 13 because of a recent fight.

Typical RPG Attributes could be:

- Strength
- Wisdom
- Endurance
- Speed
- Health

Attributes can also be listed as Skills in the Game Editor.

Managing the Attributes List

This area contains all the controls needed to create, delete, and manage Attributes.

Save Attributes

This button saves the current Attributes list.

Attributes Selection List

You may add up to 40 of your own attributes and / or skills to the list. Use this list to select the Attribute or Skill you are currently defining.

New Attribute

Use this button to create a new Attribute or Skill.

Remove Attribute

Use this button to remove the currently selected Attribute.

Rename Attribute

Use this button to change the name of the currently selected Attribute.

Set Fixed Attributes

The Game Editor uses some Attributes for in-game calculations. Set Fixed Attributes lets you "map" your attributes to those the Game Editor needs for internal calculations. For instance, you may have defined an Attribute called "Hit Points" to measure the relative health of a character. In this case, you would "map" Hit Points to the built-in Health Attribute so the Game Client (and the Game Server) can know when the character has died, in other words, when Hit Points (and therefore Health) has reached zero or less.

Health Selector

Use the Health selector to choose which of your defined Attributes represents Health. This is used to determine when a character has been killed.

Energy Selector

Use the Energy selector to choose which of your defined Attributes represents Energy. This is used to determine how long a character can run before resting. This is usually set to your Endurance or Constitution Attribute, but can also be set to NONE if not used.

Chapter 10: Attributes Tab

Breath Selector
Use the Breath selector to choose which of your defined Attributes represents how long a character can hold their breath. When a character becomes submerged in water the Breath Attribute is slowly diminished until the character drowns and dies. This is usually set to your Endurance or Constitution Attribute, but can also be set to NONE if not used.

Toughness Selector
Use the Toughness selector to choose which of your defined Attributes represents Toughness. Toughness is required if using the built-in combat feature. This is usually set to your Endurance or Constitution Attribute.

Strength Selector
Use the Strength Selector to choose which of your defined Attributes represents Strength. Strength is required if using the built-in combat feature. This is usually set to your Strength or Body or Physique Attribute.

Speed Selector
Use the Speed selector to control how fast a character can travel through the game environment. This is usually set to your Quickness, Velocity, or Speed Attribute.

Attribute is a Skill Option
Use this checkbox to define the Attribute as a Skill and it will be listed in the Skills section of the Character Sheet in the Game Client. Skills only show their current value on the Character Sheet in the Game Client, not the maximum value.

Hide Attribute From Players Option
This checkbox allows you to hide the Attribute or Skill from the player. Use this for things like Luck or other aspects that you don't want the player to know the current value of.

Assignable Attribute Points Available at Character Creation
This box allows you to set a number of extra points a player can use in the Character Creation screen to customize their Starting Attribute values.

Chapter 11: Actors Tab

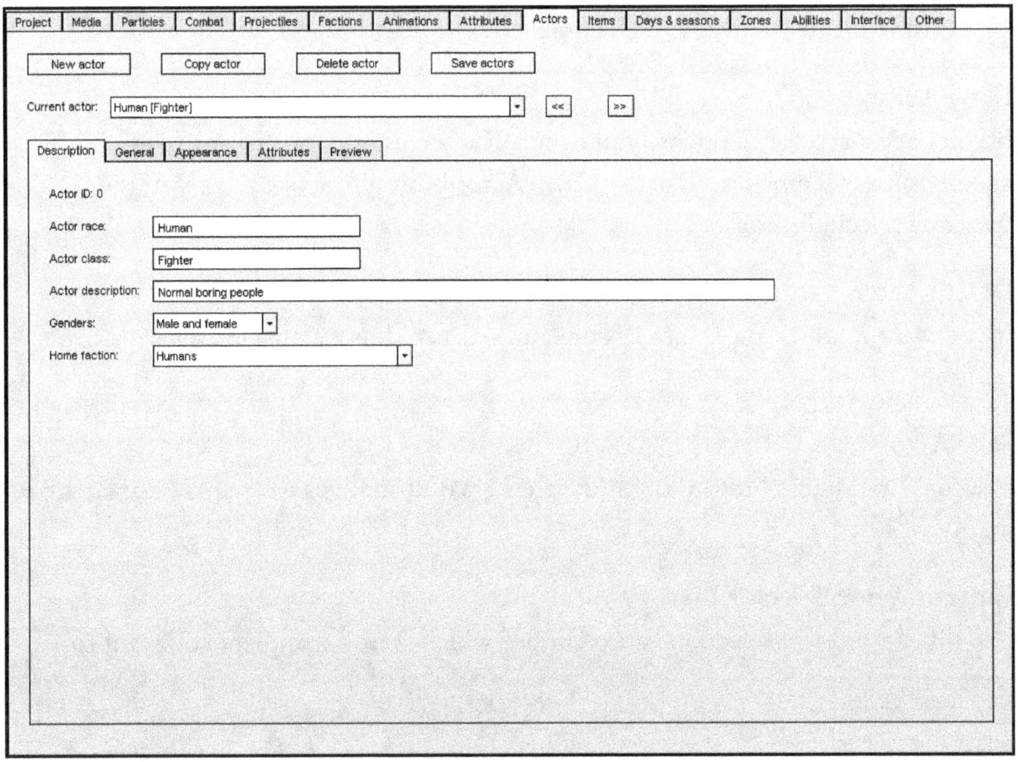

Figure 11.1 Actors Tab

Actors Tab Details

Actors are used for everything in the game that has a Life attribute. Using the Actors Tab allows you to create a selection of Actor Templates that are used by the Game Engine to create individual instances of the Actor.

For example, you could make a Human Warrior template then place human Warrior Actors around your environment to act as guards.

If you need an army, you could create a single Soldier template, then place as many as you wanted in the game.

You could make Actor Templates to represent animals, NPC's, and monsters.

Chapter 11: Actors Tab

Managing the Actors List

This area controls the creation, deletion, and management of the Actors List.

New Actor

This button creates a new Actor Template.

Copy Actor

If you have an Actor Template you have already created, you can use it as a basis for making similar templates. Use the Copy Actor button to make a copy of the currently selected Actor.

Delete Actor

If you want to destroy an Actor Template, you can do so with the Delete Actor button.

Save Actors

Use the Save Actors button to immediately save all changes to Actor Templates on the Actor List.

Current Actor Selector List

Use this drop down selection list to choose which Actor Template you want to work on.

Arrows

The arrows let you select the next or previous Actor Template on the Actor List.

Actor Properties

This area contains all the controls required to detail your Actors.

Chapter 11: Actors Tab

Description Tab

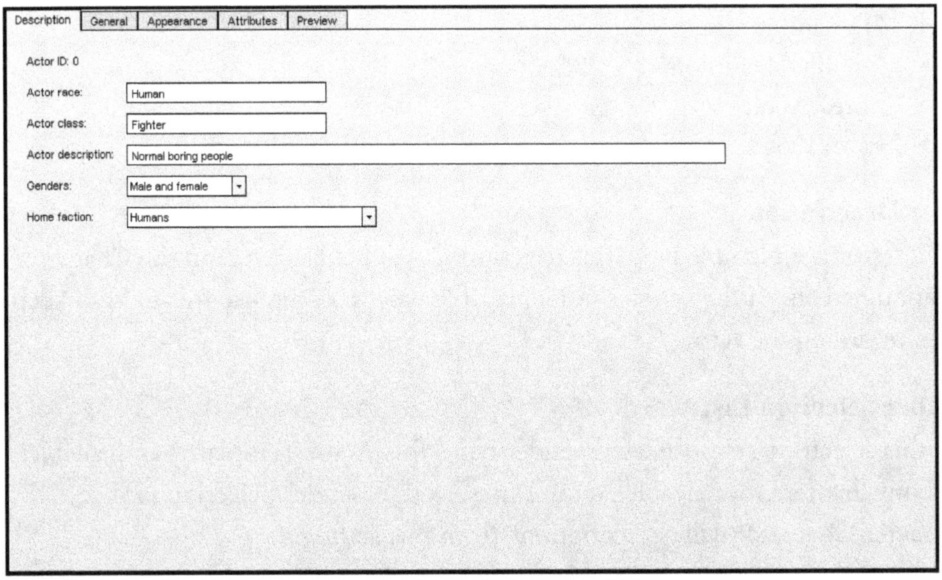

Figure 11.2 Actor Description Tab

Actor ID
Each Actor is given a unique Actor ID, which helps the Game Engine reference Actor Templates.

Actor Race
This is where you define the Race of the currently selected Actor Template. Use Race to crate groups of Actors in your game.

For instance, your game Races might be:

- Humans
- Orcs
- Forest Animals
- Farm Animals
- Aliens Races
- Goblins
-

Actor Class
Each Actor also has an Actor Class. Think of the Class as the Profession or other subset of the Race you created.

Chapter 11: Actors Tab

For example:

- Human Fighter
- Goblin Champion
- Forest Wolf
- Farm Dog

Actor Description

If the Actor is a playable type, this description will be displayed on the Character Creation Screen. If the actor is not a playable type, you can use this field to keep notes regarding the actor.

Gender Selection List

Use this selector to choose what gender types this Actor Template has available. This only matters for playable Actor Types, as the Gender Selection in the Character Generator will get its options from this setting.

- **Male and Female**- If this is chosen, the Game Editor will allow you to set a different set of 3D meshes and 2D textures for males and females.
- **Male Only**- If this is chosen, the Game Editor will allow you only one set of actor meshes for male Actors.
- **Female Only**- If this is chosen, the Game Editor will allow you only one set of actor meshes (for female Actors).
- **No Gender**- Actors set for No Gender use the actor meshes and textures listed for males.

Home Faction Selection List

If the Actor belongs to a Faction, you can choose it here.

General Tab

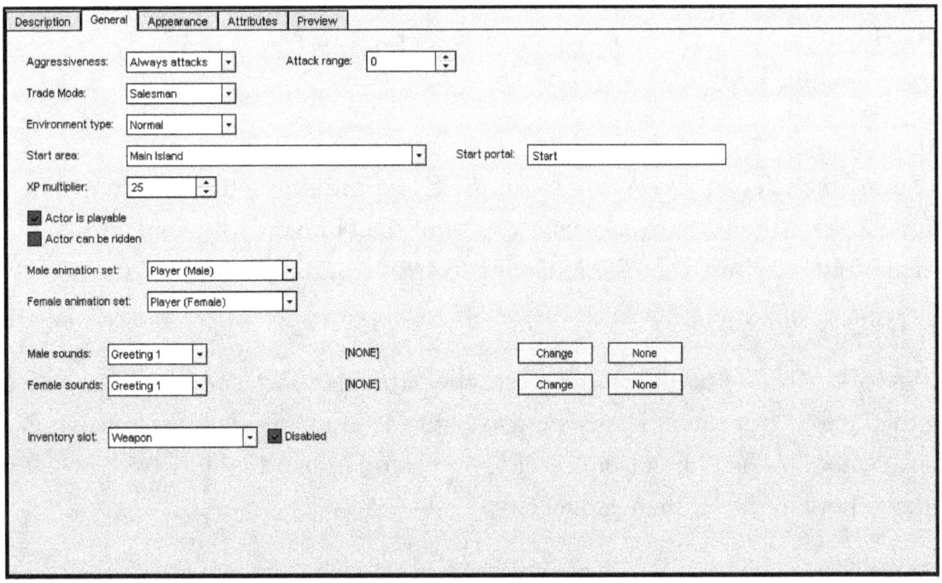

Figure 11.3 Actors General Tab

Aggressiveness Selection List
- **Passive**- Actor will not attack, even if attacked.
- **Defensive**- Actor will not attack unless attacked.
- **Always Attacks**- Actor will attack on sight and aggressively pursue enemies.
- **Non-Combatant**- Actor cannot have combat interactions at all.

Attack Range

This sets how far away an enemy has to be to activate Attack Mode. A setting of 40 gives a decent perception range.

This setting only applies to Actors that can engage in combat.

Trade Mode

This sets how the Actor can be interacted with (if it is not hostile).

- **Salesman**- Inventory items are exchanged for money.
- **Pack Animal**- Inventory items are exchanged freely.

Environment Type

What type of environment does this Actor normally move about in? Does it swim? Fly? Crawl on land? This is where you set the home environment for the Actor.

Chapter 11: Actors Tab

- **Normal**- Actor can walk and swim.
- **Swimming Only**- Actor can only move in water areas.
- **Flying**- Actor can move freely through the air.
- **Walking Only**- Actor can move on land only.

Start Area

The Start Area selector allows you to set the Zone and Portal used for spawning playable Actors. For example, maybe you want the Humans to spawn in the Human capital city, and the Elf characters to spawn in the Elf capital city.

Start Portal

The Start Portal selector allows you to set the particular portal you want associated with this Actor. For example, maybe you want the Human Wizards to spawn in a Wizard School in the Human capital city, but want Human Fighters to spawn at the Fighter School in the Human capital city.

XP Multiplier

This value is used only by the internal formula to determine automatic XP awarded from kills (if you have not defined another way to deal out XP awards). The preferred method is to calculate and assign your own XP based on your own formula.

Actor is Playable Option

Use this control to set whether or not the Actor is a playable type.

Actor Can Be Ridden Option

Use this is the Actor can be ridden by another actor. This is used for things such as horses, flying carpets, and so forth.

Male and Female Animation Set Selection List

Choose the animation set that goes along with the animated mesh for the male actor model. This list gets its entries from animations listed in the Animations Tab.

Male and Female Sounds Selection List

Assigned Sound

This is where you can assign various sounds associated with the Actor. The path to the audio file will be shown; otherwise, [NONE] is displayed.

This selector has entries for the following:

- Greeting 1
- Greeting 2
- Goodbye 1
- Goodbye 2
- Attack 1
- Attack 2
- Ouch 1
- Ouch 2
- Help!
- Death!
- Dry Footstep
- Wet Footstep

If your actor does not call for help, you can use the slot reserved for help (or any other unused audio slot) for a different sound, and then call that sound from scripting.

Change

Use this control to change the audio file assigned to the current Sound Selection.

None

Use this control to clear the audio file associated with the currently Sound Selection

Inventory Slots Selection List

This list allows you to set the available inventory slots on the Actor. For instance, if the actor is an animal and can't use a hat, then you would disable the hat inventory slot.

Inventory Slot Disabled Option

This control allows you to set the associated inventory slot as disabled.

Chapter 11: Actors Tab

Appearance Tab

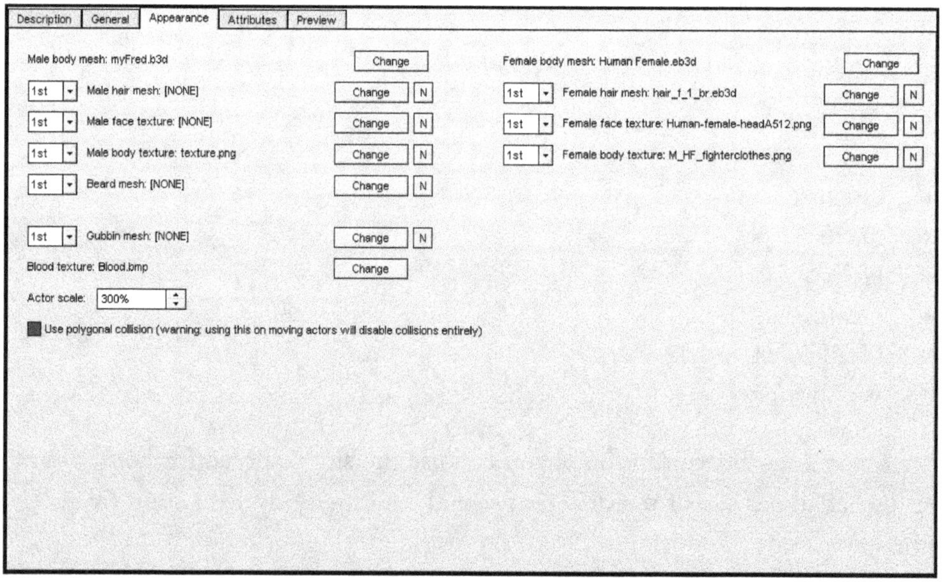

Figure 11.4 Actors Appearance Tab

The Appearance Tab is used to define how the currently selected Actor will look.

There are five slots to hold various meshes for various body parts.

Male and Female Body Mesh Selected
Use this control to select the 3D mesh that you want to use for the body model. Meshes must already be entered in the Project Media Library.

Change
Use this control to change the 3D mesh the Game Client will display for this Actor's body.

All Actors must have a body mesh of some sort; even if it is a small, transparent box.

Male and Female Hair Mesh Selection List

Currently Selected Male Hair Mesh File
This displays the currently selected mesh for the different hair styles available for this Actor.

Change

Use this control to change the 3D mesh the Game Client will display for this Actor's hair.

None

This button clears any meshes assigned to this hair slot.

Male and Female Face Texture Selection List

Currently Selected Male Face Texture File

This displays the texture file associated with the currently selected face slot.

Change

This displays the currently selected texture for the different facial skins available for this Actor.

None

This button clears any textures assigned to this face texture slot.

Male and Female Body Texture Selection List

Currently Selected Body Texture File

This displays the texture file associated with the currently selected body slot.

Change

This displays the currently selected texture for the different body skins available for this Actor.

None

This button clears any textures assigned to this body texture slot.

Beard Mesh Selection List

Beard meshes are only available for male Actors.

Currently Selected Beard Mesh File

This displays the currently selected mesh for the different beard styles available for this Actor.

Change

Use this control to change the 3D mesh the Game Client will display for this Actor's beard.

Chapter 11: Actors Tab

None
This button clears any meshes assigned to this beard slot.

Gubbin Mesh Selection List
You can add 3D meshes to any of the 6 moving body Gubbins to add decoration to your Actor. For instance, maybe the Human Soldier and the Human Guard use the same model. You could add meshes for specialized equipment to the soldier, such as armored bracers. Keep in mind this is for cosmetics only and does not necessarily reflect what is in the Actor's Inventory.

Currently Selected Gubbin Mesh File
Gubbin slots are numbered 1 through 6 and correspond to the following:

- Gubbin 1- L_Shoulder
- Gubbin 2- R_Shoulder
- Gubbin 3- L_Forearm
- Gubbin 4- R_ Forearm
- Gubbin 5- L_Shin
- Gubbin 6- R_Shin

Change
Use this control to change the mesh associated with the currently selected Gubbin slot.

None
This clears any meshes loaded into this Gubbin slot.

Blood Texture Selected
This is the texture used for blood spray. The default is the red blood texture.

Change
Use this control to change the blood texture for the selected Actor.

Actor Scale
This control allows you to change the size of the Actor model. Sometimes you will need this to make minor adjustments to how models have been exported from modeling software and imported into the Project Media Library. Sometimes you may just want to use a larger version of the same Actor for something else, like making a Human actor and setting it to be 3 times larger to make it a giant.

Use Polygonal Collision Option

This allows you to set the collision area of the Actor. If the Actor is a strange shape, and stationary, you might want to set the collision to polygonal. However, this option can cause a performance hit so use sparingly. Also, note that if applied to an animated Actor, no collision detection will occur at all.

Starting Gear

Sometimes you want your monsters or players to have some free starter gear. For players, you would typically give them a starter sword and very basic armor. For monsters, a Town Guard, for instance, you want them to spawn with a set of armor and weapons typical to their Class. In this case, maybe a decent sword and armor provided by the town would be appropriate.

Starting gear is created in the Items Tab and put into an Actor's inventory using scripting.

The best place to put a script for Player starter gear is in the Login.rsl script located here:
<projectName>\Data\Server Data\Scripts

The Login script is automatically run once each time a Player logs onto the game. We could write a Login script that checks to see if the character is new, and assign him some starter gear.

Open Login.rsl in a text editor and enter the following:

Chapter 11: Actors Tab

Listing 11.1   Login.rsl - **Starter gear for new characters.**

```
Using "RC_Core.rcm"

Function Main()
       ; get player id
       Player% = Actor()

       ; get current XP
       Result% = ActorXP(Player)

       ; check to see if player is new
       if Result = 0 then
              ; player is new - give him a rusty sword
              GiveItem(Player, "Rusty Sword", 1)

              ; give player some XP so starting gear wont
              ; be given twice
              GiveXP(Player, 1)
       endif
End Function
```

So what's happening here? Well, we are checking to see if the Actor is a new player with no XP. If the player has no XP, give her a rusty sword and one XP. The next time the Player logs on, they will have more than zero XP and so will not receive any starter gear.

Giving starter gear to monsters is a little trickier. Monsters are spawned from waypoints, so the script that gives them items must be started from the waypoint.

In our example, we want to spawn a Town Guard and give him a Fine Sword and Leather Chest Armor.

Open a text editor and enter the following:

Chapter 11: Actors Tab

Listing 11.2   TownGuardSetup.rsl - **Starter gear for new NPC.**

```
Using "RC_Core.rcm"
Function Main()
      ; get id number for Guard
      Guard% = Actor()

      ; put items in guards inventory
      GiveItem(Guard, "Fine Sword", 1)
      GiveItem(Guard, "Leather Chest Armor", 1)
End Function
```

Be sure to save this file as TownGuardSetup.rsl inside the following folder: <projectName>\Data\Server Data\Scripts

Now open the Game Editor and go to the Zone you want to spawn your monster in. Place a waypoint just above the ground (place it too low and the monster will spawn below the terrain and fall forever).

Under the Spawn this Actor drop-down, choose Town Guard.

Under the Spawn Script drop-down, choose TownGuardSetup.

When the Town Guard spawns, he will be wearing the armor and carrying the sword.

Chapter 11: Actors Tab

Attributes Tab

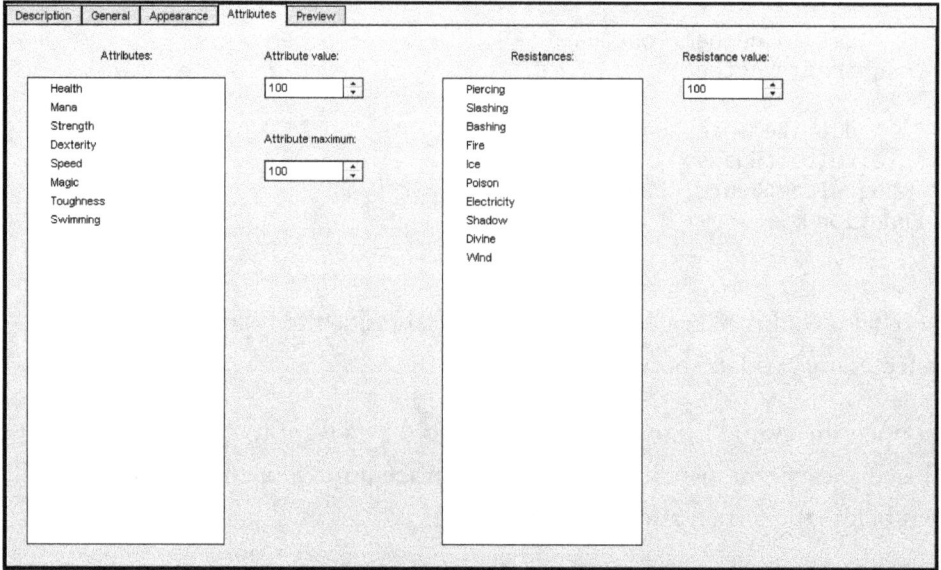

Figure 11.5 Actors Attributes Tab

Use the Attributes Tab to set the various Attribute scores for this Actor Template. Attributes are created in the Attributes Tab.

Attributes Selection List
Use this control to select the Attribute you wish to modify for this Actor Template.

Usually the Current and Maximum would be set to the same amount, unless you want your Actor to spawn as partially damaged for some reason.

Attribute Value (Current)
This controls the value of the Attribute when the Actor is spawned.

This value can also be manipulated during the game through scripting.

Attribute Maximum
This controls the maximum value an Actor can have in an Attribute when it spawns.

This value can also be manipulated during the game through scripting.

Resistances (to Damage Types)

Is this Actor fireproof? Is it really tough? Use the Resistances to give your Actor natural (or supernatural) resistances to certain types of damage.

Resistance Value

The higher the value, the more the Actor will be resistant to that type of damage.

Values must be a positive integer.

Chapter 11: Actors Tab

Preview Tab

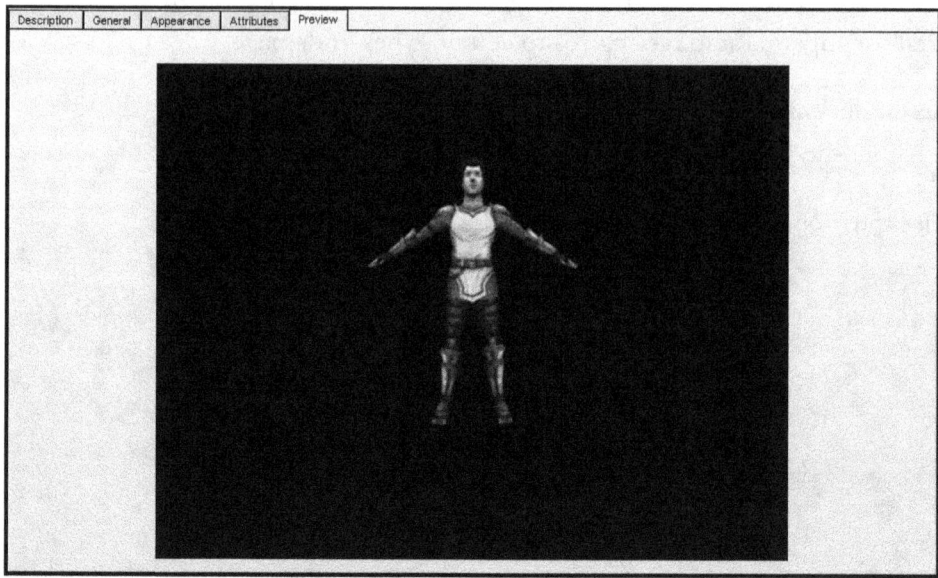

Figure 11.6 Actors Preview Tab

This tab displays a 3D preview of the Actor. The model view can be rotated using the mouse. To rotate, hold down the left mouse button and drag the mouse.

Chapter 12: Items Tab

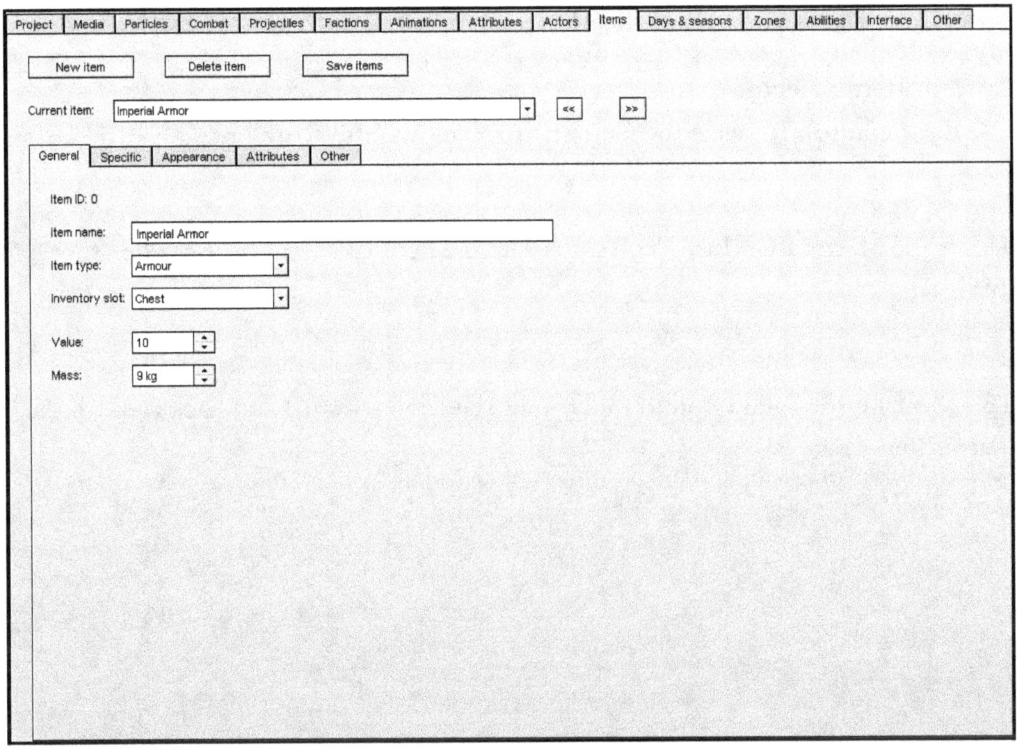

Figure 12.1 Items Tab

Items Tab Details

Every RPG needs some kind of items; from armor to swords, potions to laser guns, items are the pieces of treasure, maps, and equipment the player is adventuring for.

Use the Item Tab to create all the in-game items you need to arm and equip characters and NPC's.

Managing the Items List

This area contains all the controls required to create, delete, and manage all the Items in the game.

New Item

This button allows you to create a new Item in the Master Item List.

Chapter 12: Items Tab

Delete Item

This button allows you to delete the Item from the Master Item List.

Save Item

This button allows you to save the Master Item List.

Current Item Selector

Use these controls to select the Current Item you wish to work on.

List

This is the Master Item List. You can select the item you want to focus on from this list.

<< and >>

The arrow buttons allow you to move your selection forward and backward on the Master Item List.

Chapter 12: Items Tab

General Tab

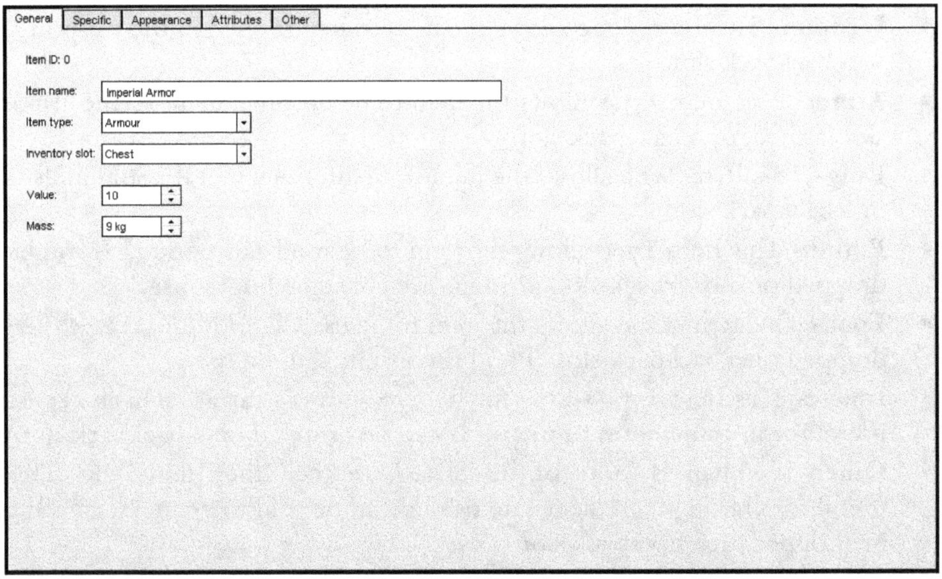

Figure 12.2 Items General Tab

Item ID

This is the internal ID number given to the Item by the Game Editor when the Item is first created.

Item Name

This is the name of the Item as you wish it to appear in-game.

Item Type

An Item may be of a specific subtype. The subtypes allow further customization of the Item and how it is handled in the Game Client.

Chapter 12: Items Tab

Item Types:

- **Weapon-** This Item Type allows the item to be dropped in the weapon slot or a backpack slot.
- **Armor-** This Item Type allows the item to be dropped in a specific armor slot (armed) or a backpack slot.
- **Ring-** This Item Type allows the item to be dropped in a ring or amulet slot or a backpack slot.
- **Potion-** This Item Type allows the item to be used as a potion. It can be dropped on a backpack slot. Potions are consumed upon use.
- **Food-** This Item Type allows the item to be used as food. It can be dropped on a backpack slot. Food is consumed upon use.
- **Image-** This Item Type allows the item to show an image. This is especially useful for in-game notes or maps. It can be dropped on a backpack slot.
- **Other-** If an item is "none of the above", use the Other Item Type. This is useful for crafting ingredients, items that can be sold to vendors, etc. It can be dropped on a backpack slot.

Inventory Slot

Use this selector to choose which inventory slot (other than backpack) the Item belongs to in order to wear it, arm it, or equip it.

Value

This represents how much the Item is worth. Value is given as Base Units (see Other Tab).

Mass

If you want to keep track of how big or heavy something is, you can use the Mass field. If you are not using mass in your game, you can use this field to hold other information.

Specific Tab

This tab allows the user to enter details that are specific to the type of item selected on the Item Type drop-down.

Chapter 12: Items Tab

Weapon Specifics

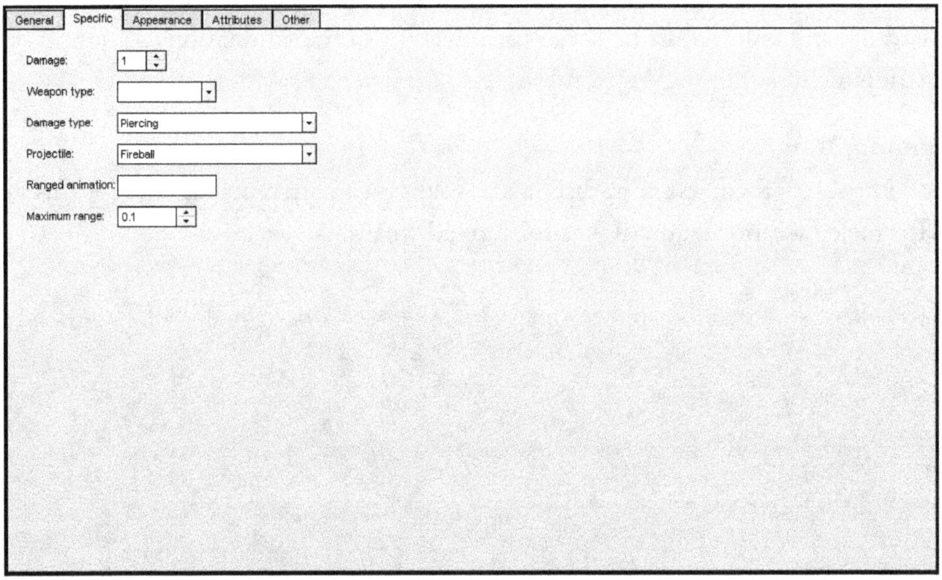

Figure 12.3 Item Weapon Specifics Tab

This is the section where you detail weapon specifics.

Damage
This controls how many points of damage the weapon does when it successfully hits an unarmored target.

Weapon Type
This section defines what type of weapon we are creating.

- **One Handed** - Use this for weapons such as daggers, pistols, short swords, etc.
- **Two Handed** - Use this for weapons such as pole arms, spears, great swords, etc.
- **Ranged** - Use this for weapons such as grenades, crossbows, guns, throwing knives, etc.

Projectile
If the weapon shoots a projectile, such as arrows, bullets, sling stones, cannonballs, knives, etc., select the projectile type from the drop-down list. Keep in mind the projectile should be set up in the Projectiles Tab.

Chapter 12: Items Tab

Ranged Animation

Enter the name of the animation you want to be associated with this weapon. Keep in mind the animation must be setup for the actor in the Animations Tab (and be an animation included on the Actor mesh).

Maximum Range

This control sets the maximum distance a weapon can strike its target. Set this very low for melee weapons, and higher for ranged weapons.

Armor Specifics

Figure 12.4 Items Armor Specifics Tab

This section allows you to setup information specific to armor items.

Armor Level
This spinner is used to indicate the relative protection level of this piece of armor. Lower numbers indicate less protection, higher numbers indicate more protection.

Ring Specifics
There are no detail entries for rings at this time.

Chapter 12: Items Tab

Potion Specifics

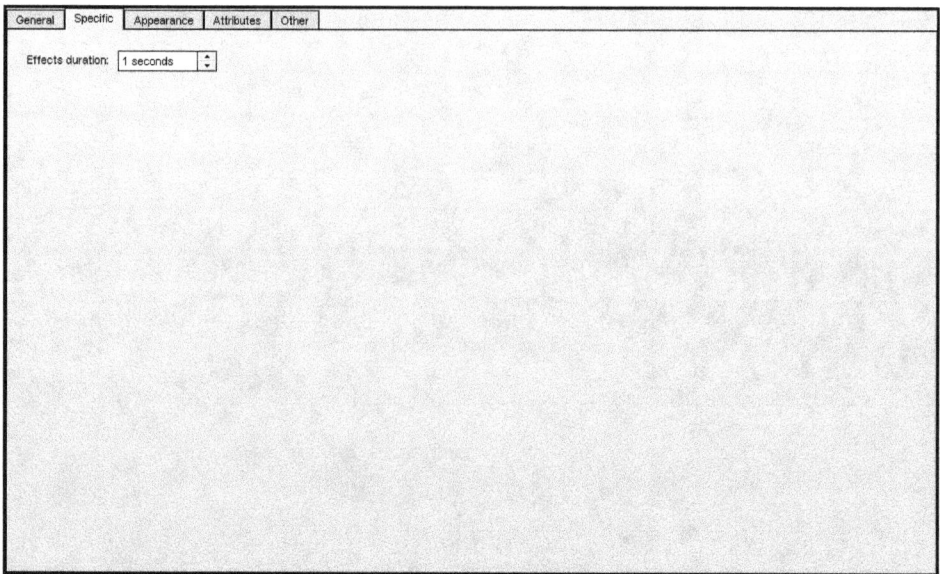

Figure 12.5 Items Potion Specifics

Use this area to define how specific potions work. Potions can be anything from the classic flasks and beakers of dungeon crawls or could be any other consumable item, such as hypo-sprays, stim-doses, med packs, or whatever.

Effects Duration

This spinner sets the duration on the effects granted by consuming the Potion in seconds.

Food Specifics

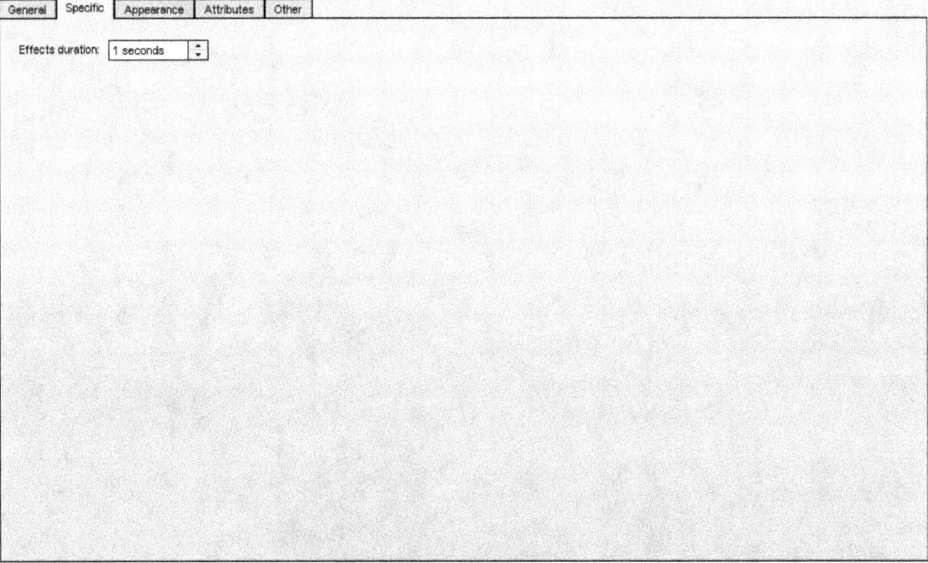

Figure 12.5 Items Food Specifics Tab

This section is used to detail the specific types of food or drink used in the game. You can use this for regular things, such as food and water, or use it creatively to represent pills, med kits, or many other items that are consumed on use. Note this works the same as Potions, but gives an extra category for similar consumables.

Effects Duration

This spinner sets the duration on the effects granted by consuming the Food in seconds.

Chapter 12: Items Tab

Image Specifics

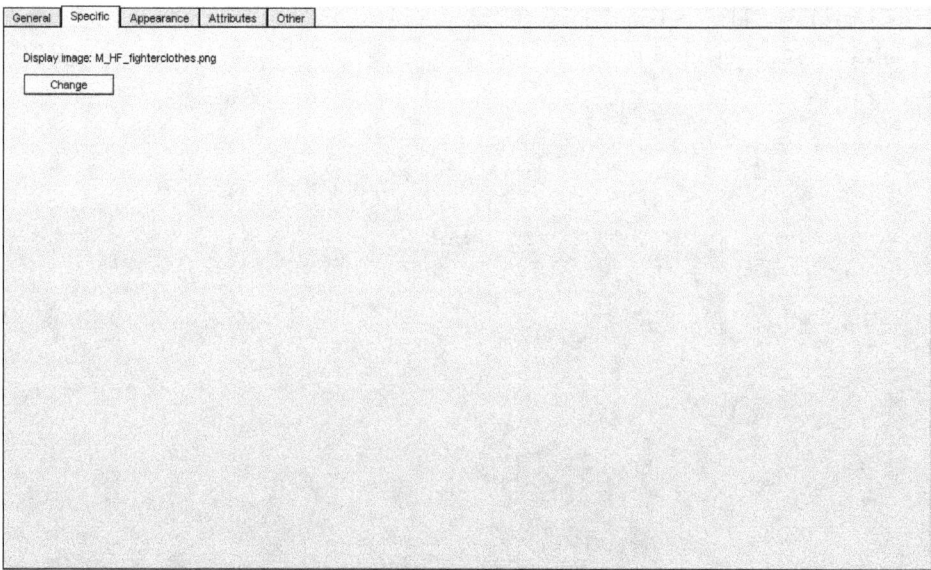

Figure 12.6 Items Image Specifics Tab

This section is used to define images that can be displayed in-game. This is normally used for things such as hand-written notes the player may wish to consult or more commonly, for maps.

Display Image
Use this button to open a selector that looks into the Master Media List. Keep in mind images must first be loaded into the Master Media List through the Media tab.

Other Specifics

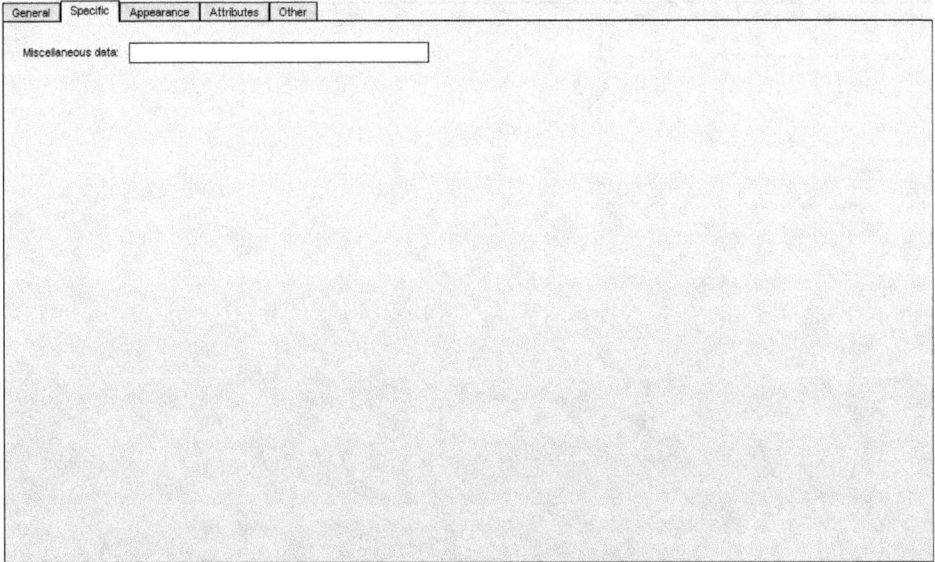

Figure 12.7 Items Other Specifics Tab

Use this section to define items that do not easily fit into other categories.

Miscellaneous Data
This box can hold a string of information that can be later decoded through scripting.

Chapter 12: Items Tab

Appearance Tab

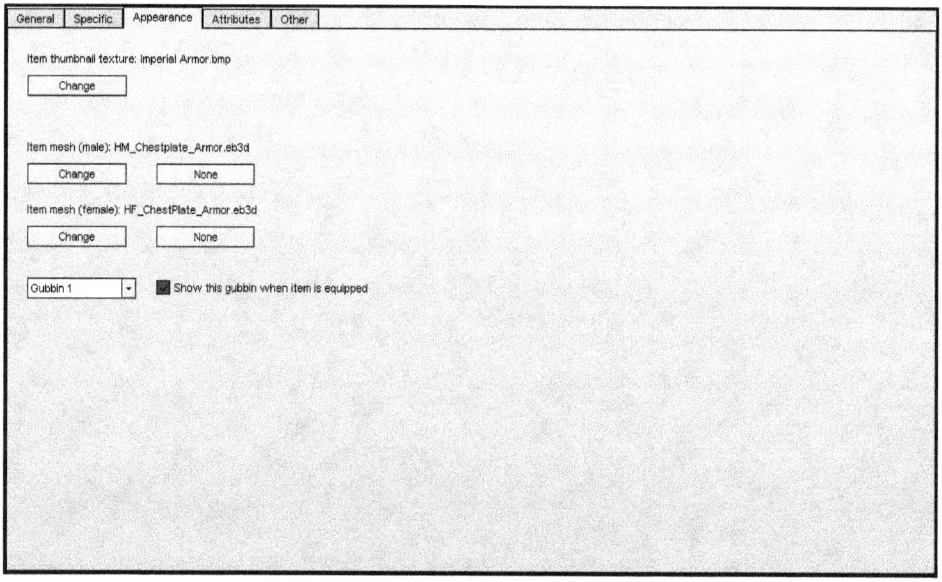

Figure 12.8 Items Appearance Tab

Item Thumbnail Texture

This button opens a selector view of the Master Media List. Use this to select the thumbnail you wish to use as the icon for this item. Keep in mind the icon must be already loaded into the Master Media List via the Media Tab.

A good size for thumbnails is 50 x 50 pixels, but the image should also look good at 80 x 80 pixels (this is the size the item is resized to when you pick it up in the inventory screen).

Item Mesh (Male / Female)

You can make a separate mesh for male or female actors. This button will open a selector into the Master Media List, so keep in mind that the mesh must already be loaded via the Media tab. If you don't want to use a mesh, select the None button.

Gubbin Selection List

Use this selector to choose what gubbins to show when this item is equipped.

Show This Gubbin When Item Is Equipped Option

Use this control along with the Gubbin Selection List to turn on certain gubbins when this item is equipped.

Chapter 12: Items Tab

Attributes Tab

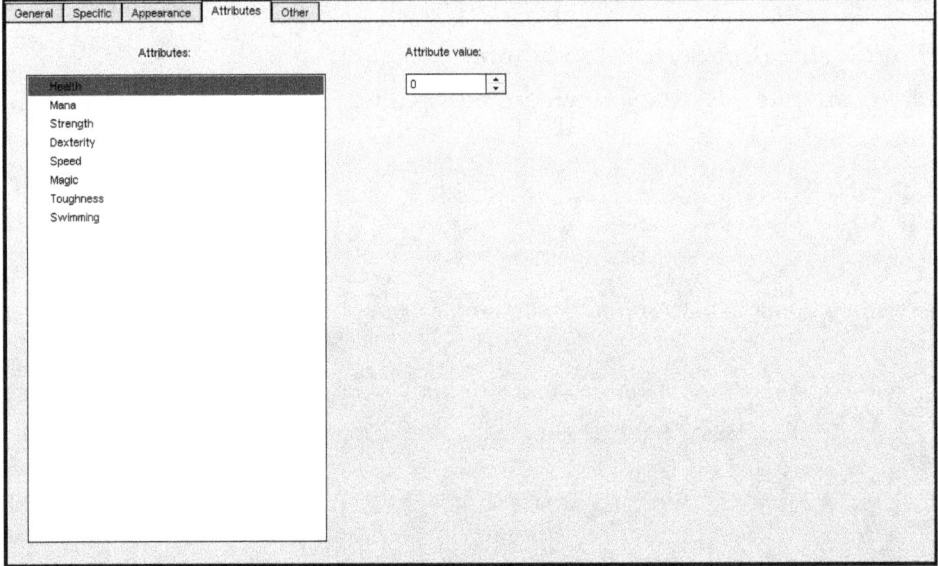

Figure 12.9 Items Attributes Tab

This section allows you to set the various Attributes of the item. Using this section, you can apply bonuses and penalties for various types of items. For instance, if you want a piece of armor to add 5 points of Strength, come to this tab and set Strength to 5, then write a custom script to increase the Strength attribute.

For creating potions, set the item type to "potion", and then set the effect duration, next set the attributes you want to effect. The Game Editor's built-in script will run when the potion is used. For example, we create a Health Potion item, set its type to "potion", set the duration for 5 seconds, and set the Health attribute to 10. When the player uses the potion in-game, the automatic item script for potions will run, destroying 1 unit of Health Potion from the Actor's inventory, and causing the Actor's Health to increase by 10 for 5 seconds.

** Note- for items that must be worn in order to gain any effect you will have to write a script in Equip Change.rsl that applies or takes away the effects. To do this, check what item is in each slot and apply its bonuses or penalties, which are set in the Items> Attributes Tab. The Equip Change.rsl script is run every time the user adds or removes worn items (also called "(un)equipping an item").

Chapter 12: Items Tab

Attributes Selection List

Use this list to select the Attributes you want to set for this item.

Attribute Value (For Selected Attribute)

For each Attribute selected, you can use this spinner to set the value you want for that attribute.

Other Tab

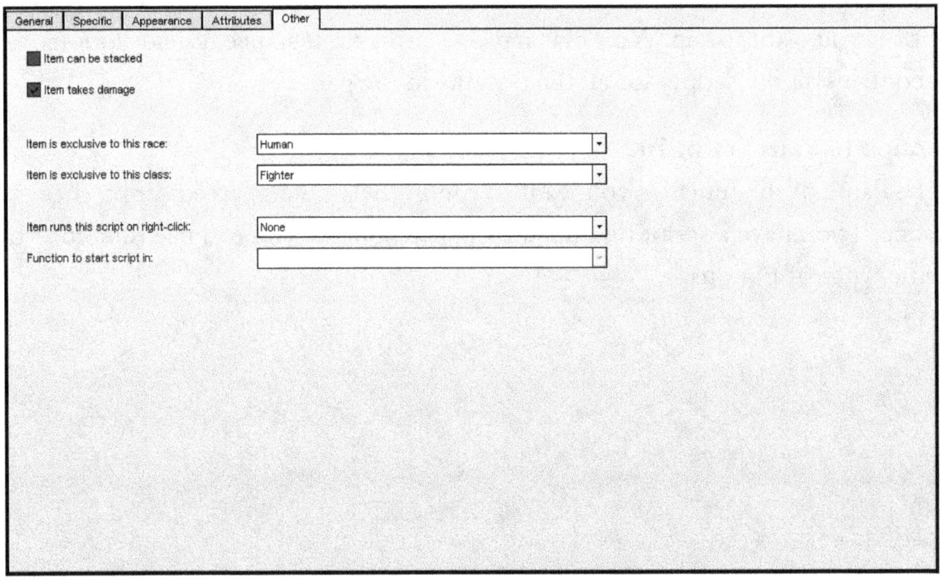

Figure 12.10 Items Other Tab

This tab allows control of such things as whether or not an item can be stacked, if an item can only be used by a specific race, and other options.

Item Can Be Stacked Option
Select this option if you want to allow the user to stack items in their backpack. The maximum number of items allowed in a stack is 65,535. If you go beyond this amount by adding two stacks together, the total will wrap around. In other words, if you add a stack of 10 to a stack of 65,535, you will end up with one stack of 9.

Item Takes Damage Option
Select this option if you want the item to take damage from combat.

Item is Exclusive to the Race Selection
If the item is only used by a specific race, select the race from the drop-down menu, otherwise select None.

Item is Exclusive to this Class Selection
If the item is only to be used by a specific class, select the class from the drop-down menu, otherwise select None.

Chapter 12: Items Tab

Item Runs This Script on Right Click

If you want to run a custom script when the item is "used", enter the name of the script file you want to run. You may have a script, for instance, called Potions.rsl that contains all the scripts for all the potions in the game.

Function to Start Script In

Set the name of the function you want to run in the above selected script. For instance, if you have a script that handles all the potions, you can use functions for specific types of potions.

Chapter 13: Days & Seasons Tab

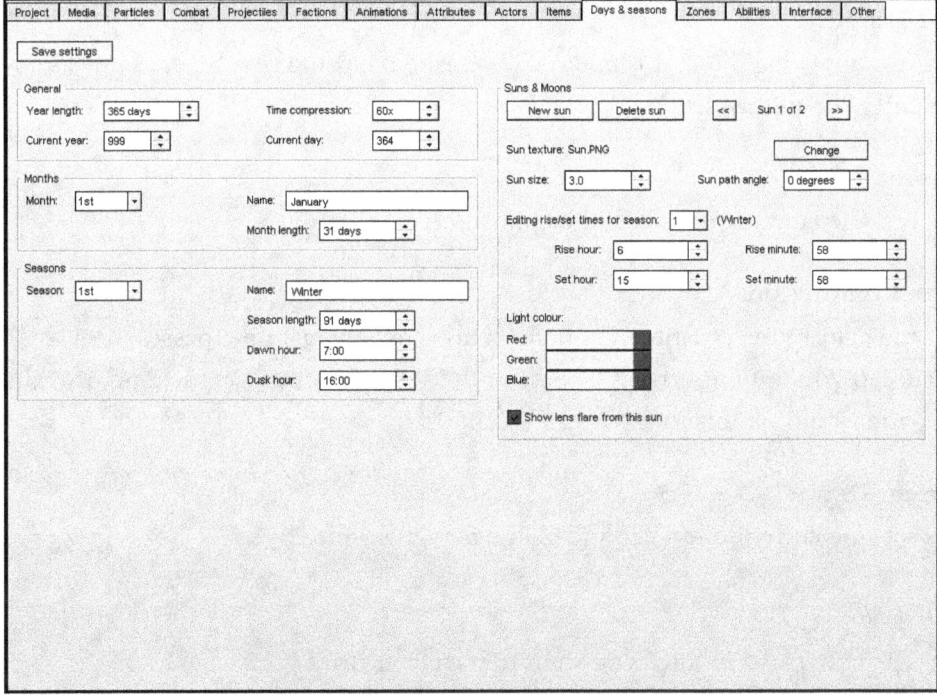

Figure 13.1 Days and Seasons Tab

Days & Seasons Tab Details

The Days & Seasons Tab is used to define the global game environment. This is where you control the length of day and night, the seasons, and the number of days in a year. You can also create custom day and month names and change what the sun and moon look like.

If you are using trees created with the RC Tree Creator, the leaves can change color depending on the season. In order to do this you must use grayscale textures for the leaves. Remember, textures and meshes must be loaded into the Master Media List through the Media Tab.

Save Settings

This button saves the current Days & Seasons settings.

Chapter 13: Days & Seasons Tab

General

The General Tab is where basic time and calendar info is defined for the game world.

Year Length

This sets how long the year is in days. To make the game year be the same as a real year enter 365 in this field.

Current Year

This sets the current year when the Game Server is started.

Time Compression

You can adjust time compression here. This sets how fast time passes. For instance, if you want 6 seconds to pass in the game for every one second of real time, you would set this to 6.

Current Day

This sets the current day when the Game Server is started.

Months

This sets how many months you want to have in a year.

Month Selection List

Use this list to select the current month.

Name of Month

This is the name of the currently selected month.

Month Length

This is how long months are in days.

Seasons

Seasons can be customized to your specifications. Maybe your world has a long winter and short summer. Maybe it is always winter on your world.

Season Selection List

This list lets you select which season you want to work on.

Chapter 13: Days & Seasons Tab

Name of Season

You can name your seasons whatever you want.

Season Length

This lets you set the length of each season in days.

Dawn Hour

This sets what time of day the sun rises, set in 24-hour time.

Dusk Hour

This sets what time of day the sun sets, set in 24-hour time.

Suns & Moons

Suns and moons are defined in the same way.

To simulate a planet with 2 suns, just create 2 suns and use sun graphics.

To simulate a planet with 1 sun and 1 moon, just create 2 suns; use a sun graphic for the first sun and use a moon graphic for the second (and subsequent 'suns').

To simulate a planet with 1 sun and 2 moons, just create 3 'suns'; use a sun graphic for the first sun and use a moon graphic for the second and third 'suns'.

New Sun

Use this button to create a new sun object.

Delete Sun

Use this button to delete the currently selected sun.

Sun Selector Arrows

Use these arrow buttons to move forward and backward along the Sun List.

Currently Selected Sun

This is the sun that is currently selected. All information currently displayed is for this sun.

Sun Texture

This displays the filename of the texture of the currently selected sun.

Chapter 13: Days & Seasons Tab

Change

Use this button to bring up a file selector to change the texture of the currently selected sun.

Sun Size

This control allows you to increase or decrease the size of the sun. The default is 3 for the sun and 4 for the moon.

Sun Path Angle

This is a misnomer. This control does not set the sun's path, but rather sets where the sun / moon will rise and set.

The sun / moon are centered overhead at midday no matter the path angle set.

Set at 0 degrees, the sun / moon rises in the east and sets in the west.

Set at 45 degrees, the sun / moon rises in the northeast and sets in the southwest.

Set at 90 degrees, the sun / moon rises in the north and sets in the south.

Editing Rise / Set Times for Season Selection List

Use this selection list to choose the season you want to set the rise and set hours for.

Rise Hour

This sets the hour the sun rises each day during the currently selected season.

Rise Minute

This sets the minute the sun rises during the currently selected season.

Set Hour

This sets the hour the sun sets each day during the currently selected season.

Set Minute

This sets the minute the sun sets each day during the currently selected season.

Light Color

This allows you to set a custom color for the light coming from the sun.

Use the Red, Green, Blue sliders to adjust the color of the light.

Chapter 13: Days & Seasons Tab

Show Lens Flare From This Sun Option

This checkbox sets whether or not the currently selected sun creates a lens flare in the main camera view of the Game Client.

Chapter 14: Zones Tab

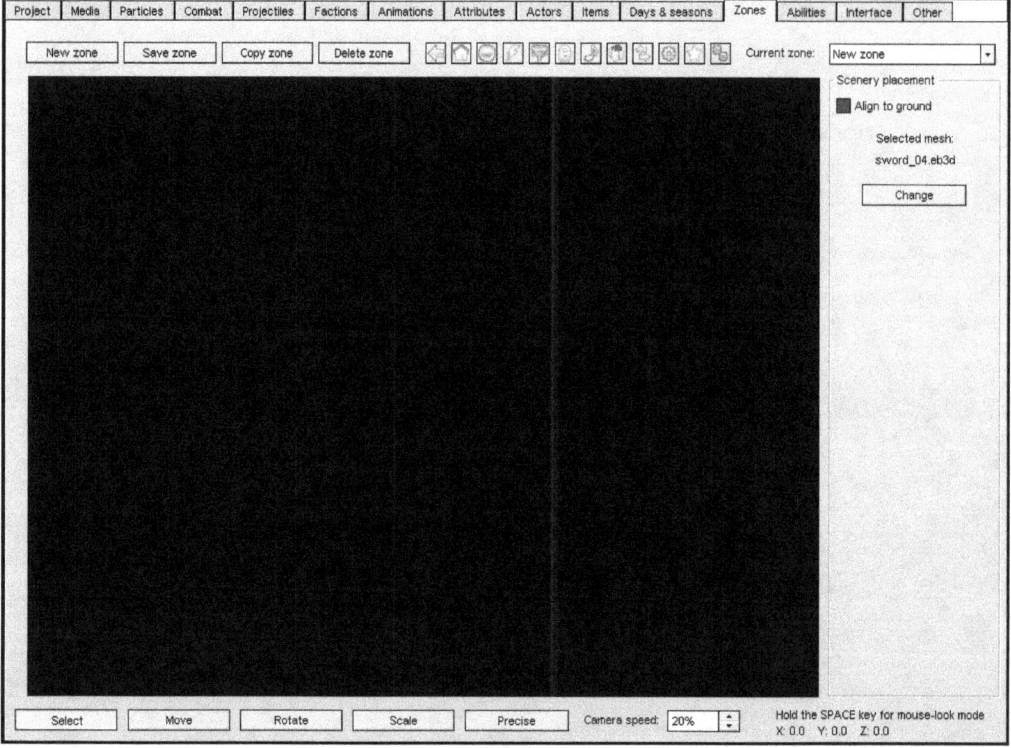

14.1 Zones Tab

Zones Tab Details

The Zones Tab is used to create physical areas within your game. These areas usually correspond to the distinct areas on your game map. Zones can be as small as a single room or as big as a continent.

Some examples of Zones:

- Tavern (small Zone)
- Room at the Inn (small Zone)
- Farm House (Small Zone)
- Jail Cell (small Zone)
- Haunted Forest (medium Zone)
- Pirate Isle (medium Zone)
- Cave Complex (medium Zone)

- Kingdom (large Zone)
- City (large Zone)
- Frontier (large Zone)

The size of a zone is relative, but with clever model scaling, sectioning, and mapping, you can simulate most areas by using Zones.

Keep in mind that zones can have Instances. Instances refer to virtual copies of the Zone. Instances are used to keep the number of players below a certain amount, as well as for creating areas that groups of players can go to that are restricted to other players.

For example, suppose you had a dungeon near a town. Well, players would find out about it and be constantly raiding it, leaving it empty most of the time. It would be better in this case to create Instances of the dungeon, this way each group of players could have access to the dungeon all to themselves without worrying other players are coming in and grabbing treasure or killing monsters ahead of them.

Zone Management

These control the creation, deletion, and management of Zones in your game.

Current Zone Selection List

Use this list to select the zone you want to work on.

New Zone

This button creates a new Zone. Be sure to immediately use the Save Zone command to name your new Zone. Zones can be deleted at any time.

Save Zone

This button saves the Zone and all its contents. Be sure to save your work often and practice some form of version control to avoid losing your work. Adding zone details, buildings, trees, and scenery can be a time-consuming process; you don't want to lose your hard work.

Copy Zone

This makes a copy of the currently selected zone. You are prompted to name the new Zone.

Copying a Zone is a great way to make alternate versions of a zone. For example, suppose you want your Zone to be snow-covered in winter. You could create a

Chapter 14: Zones Tab

summer version of the Zone, then copy the zone and substitute snow covered ground and building textures. You would then write a script that would send players to the proper zone depending on the calendar.

Delete Zone

Use this to get rid of zones you don't want to use any more. Keep in mind there is no undo for this.

Undo

If you make a mistake during the construction of your Zone, you can use the Undo button to reverse the last command.

Zone Preview Window

This window shows the current state of your Zone, and allows you to move a virtual camera around the Zone and interact with Zone content.

To rotate the camera, hold down the spacebar and move your mouse.

To move the camera forward, hold down the spacebar and the left mouse button.

To move camera backward, hold down the spacebar and the right mouse button.

Use the Camera Speed control to adjust the camera velocity.

Select

This lets you select objects relevant to the currently selected mode.

For instance, in Scenery Mode this puts you into Selection mode to select scenery objects in the currently selected Zone. If you are in Sound Zone Mode this puts you into Selection mode to select Sound Zones in the currently selected zone.

Selection is done by clicking the desired object with the mouse.

Deleting Objects

Delete objects by selecting them, then pressing the Delete key.

Move

Click this to set the currently selected object into Move mode. The object can then be moved in real time using the mouse. Hold down the left mouse button to move the selected object. When done moving the object, right click to deselect it.

Keep in mind, when in Move mode, right clicking without an object already selected will create a new object.

Rotate

This button allows you to rotate an object around its Y axis.

To rotate an object: select it with left-click, choose Rotate, then hold down the left mouse button and adjust the rotation in real time with the mouse.

Keep in mind: when in Rotate mode, right clicking without an object already selected will create a new object.

Scale

This button allows you to scale an object along all three axes (proportional scaling).

To scale an object: select it with left-click, choose Scale, then hold down the left mouse button and adjust the scale with your mouse in real time.

Keep in mind, when in Scale mode, right clicking without an object already selected will create a new object.

Chapter 14: Zones Tab

Precise

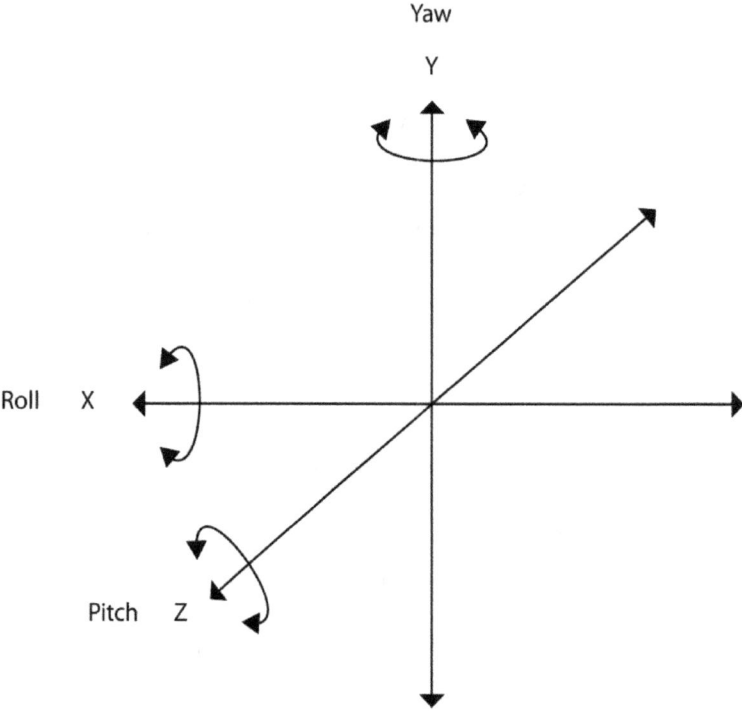

Figure 14.2 Axes of 3D Space

This button allows you to have exact control over various aspects of the currently selected object.

- Position X: The object's current position on the X axis (left to right).
- Position Y: The object's current position on the Y axis (up and down).
- Position Z: The object's current position on the Z axis (front to back)
- Pitch: Rotation around the Z axis.
- Yaw: Rotation around the Y axis.
- Roll: Rotation around the X axis.
- Scale X: Scale the object along its X axis.
- Scale Y: Scale the object along its Y axis.
- Scale Z: Scale the object along its Z axis.

Camera Speed

Adjust the camera speed to move quickly across large zones, or slowly for movement that is more precise.

X, Y, Z Camera Coordinates

These are the current coordinates of the camera. This can be useful for locating key areas of your zone that need further work or have certain geographical features.

Moving the Camera

Spacebar and Mouse

Spacebar activates camera fly mode. Hold the spacebar down while moving the mouse or using the mouse buttons to control camera movement through the Zone.

To move the camera forward, in the direction it is looking, hold down the spacebar and press the left mouse button. To move the camera backwards, hold down the spacebar while pressing the right mouse button.

Chapter 14: Zones Tab

Mode Selection Buttons

Figure 14.3 Zone Mode Selection Buttons

Zone Editing Mode Button Details

Undo	**Undo** Use this tool to reverse any mistakes you made.
Scenery	**Scenery** Use this tool to place buildings, trees, and other props within the zone. Scenery is normally aligned with the ground, but doesn't have to be.
Terrain	**Terrain** Use this tool to create the landscape for the zone. Terrain height maps and color maps can be imported.
Emitter	**Emitters** Use this tool to create particle emitters in the Zone. Emitters are used to simulate everything from waterfalls to swarms of bugs.
Water	**Water** Use this tool to place water planes within the Zone. Water planes can represent lava, water, ooze, and more.
Collision Box	**Collision Box** Use this tool to restrict Actor movement within the Zone.

Zone Editing Mode Button Details (continued)

	Trigger	
Trigger	Use this tool to designate areas in the Zone that should trigger scripts when Actors move inside them, to make special programmed events occur. Triggers can be used to simulate traps, to summon enemy monsters, and to simulate a variety of beneficial or harmful effects, such as healing areas or banners that sap player's morale. Areas could be setup to simulate faster or slower travel, such as muddy areas that decrease your movement speed.	
Waypoint	**Waypoint** Use this tool to define Actor movement routes. Waypoints can represent patrol routes for guards, or paths for monsters to walk. This could also be used for paths NPC Actors follow as they do their business in the Zone.	
Portal	**Portal** Use this tool to define Portals in the Zone. Portals are used to transport Actors to other areas in the same Zone or to other Zones.	
Environment	**Environment** Use this tool to set Environmental conditions within the Zone.	
Other	**Other** Use this tool to define miscellaneous information, such as Zone Loading Screens, Zone Scripts, and Zone Loading Music.	

Chapter 14: Zones Tab

Scenery Mode

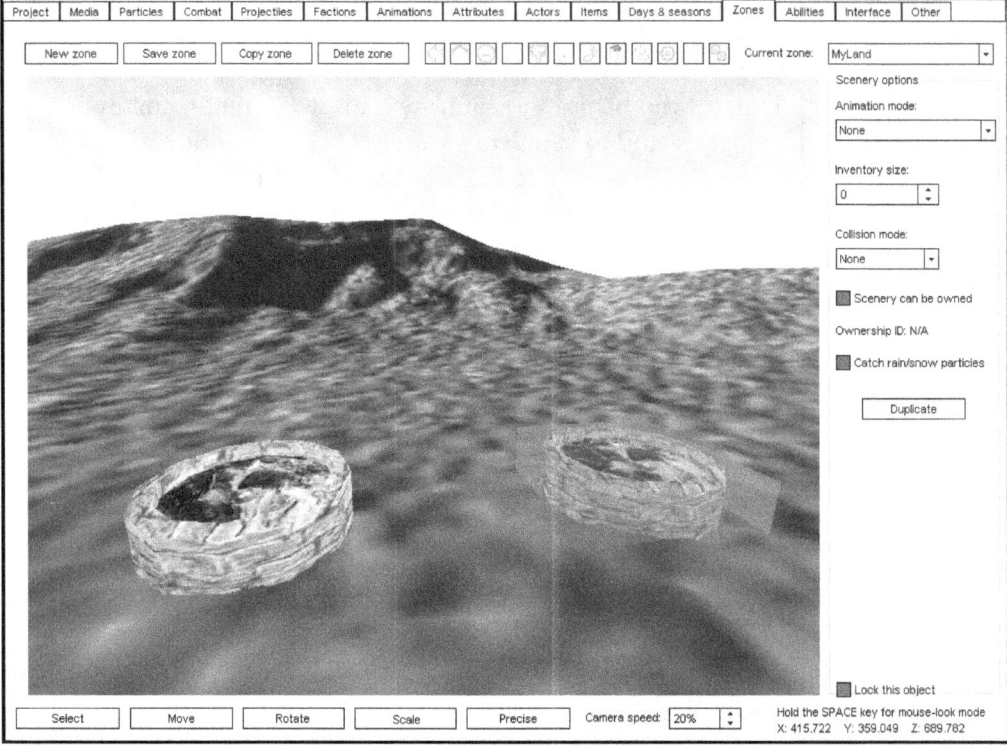

Figure 14.4 Examples of Unselected and Selected Scenery Objects (a Forge)

Scenery objects must be already loaded into the Main Media library via the Media Tab in the Game Editor.

Right-clicking in the preview screen will cause a new copy of whatever mesh is currently selected to be created. Be aware that sometimes items may not be in the correct scale for the world, they might be very small. If you don't see the model, try zooming in to locate it, and then Scale it up.

To change the currently selected mesh, right click with any mesh selected or select any of the other tools then come back to Scenery mode.

Scenery Placement
Scenery can be placed by using any of the Movement Options below the Preview Window. Use Select and Move to get your models roughly in the right place, then you can use the Precise controls to fine tune it.

Align to Ground Option

This causes scenery to snap to the ground. You may still need to use Precise adjustments.

Currently Selected Mesh

This is the filename of the currently selected mesh, for reference. Remember that all media, including meshes, must be imported into the Game Editor through the Media Tab.

Change

This button allows you to change the currently selected mesh.

Scenery Options

Animation Mode

Keep in mind that animated scenery needs to have at least one bone, called Head. The animation set name is not required; the frames are played back in order from start to finish.

- **None-** Scenery Object does not play its animation (or has no animation).
- **Constant Loop-** Scenery Object plays its animation from start to finish then begins again from the start.
- **Constant Ping-Pong-** Scenery Object plays its animation from first frame to last frame then from last frame to first frame, and then repeats.
- **When Selected-** Scenery Object plays its animation from start to finish when selected by the player.

Inventory Size

Scenery Items can hold Items. Increase the Inventory Size to define the amount of inventory space available in the Scenery Item.

Collision Mode

Collision Mode determines the way Actors interact with the scenery. If the scenery has a bounding box, that will block the Actor's movement.

- **None** - Actors can walk through the Scenery.
- **Sphere-** The bounding box of the scenery object is calculated as a sphere.
- **Box-** The bounding box of the scenery object is calculated as a box shape. This is used for blockish scenery, such as houses or fences. This is the fastest bounding box type to process.

- **Polygon**- The bounding box of the scenery object is calculated as a polygon. This is used for irregularly-shaped objects, but is processor intensive.

Scenery Can Be Owned Checkbox

If this is checked, the Scenery can be owned by players, in other words, Actors that "own" the Scenery can add and remove inventory from the Scenery.

Ownership ID Readout

This is the unique identifier for each ownable piece of Scenery.

Catch Rain/Snow Particles Checkbox

If this box is checked, the Scenery is "solid" to rain and snow particles, and will stop them. For instance, if you have two vendor shelters, one set for catching and one not, rain will fall through the shelter that has not been set, while the shelter that catches rain, will stop the rain from coming through the roof.

Chapter 14: Zones Tab

Terrain Mode

Terrain objects must be already loaded into the game media library via the Media Tab in the Game Editor.

Terrain Placement
Select a height map, then right-click the 3D view to place terrain.

Currently Selected Height Map
This is the filename of the currently selected height map.

Change Height Map
Use this button to change the currently selected height map.

Realm Crafter supports height maps in the following formats:

- BMP
- PNG
- JPG

Height maps represent terrain using shades of gray; the tall areas are white, the lowest areas are black. Shades of gray represent values between white and black, light gray is taller than dark gray.

Figure 14.5 Example of Grayscale Graphic Height map Converted to 3D Geometry

Reset
This clears the currently selected height map.

Chapter 14: Zones Tab

Terrain Options

Change Color Map
Use this to change the color map associated with the currently selected height map. Keep in mind the color map must already be loaded into the Media Library via the Media Tab.

The color map represents the grass, roads, etc., that are painted onto the terrain.

Change Detail Map
Use this button to change the detail map associated with the currently selected height map.

The detail map is an overlay that helps blend the color map with the height map.

The detail map is usually a tile-able grayscale "difference cloud".

Detail Map Scale
Use this control to change the detail map scale.

Maximum Triangles
This adjusts the resolution of the terrain mesh based on the height map.

Increase this value to increase the number of triangles used to create the 3D mesh. This will result in smoother hills and closer fidelity to the grayscale height map.

The lowest setting is 500 triangles

The highest setting is 50,000 triangles

Decrease this value for less polygons; making the resulting 3D mesh more jagged.

Enable Morphing
Morphing adds a small level of smoothing to the 3D mesh.

Enable Shading
The 3D mesh can have shading "baked on". Shadows are calculated based on the setting for the Sun in the Environmental Options section of the Zone Editor.

Chapter 14: Zones Tab

Emitters Mode

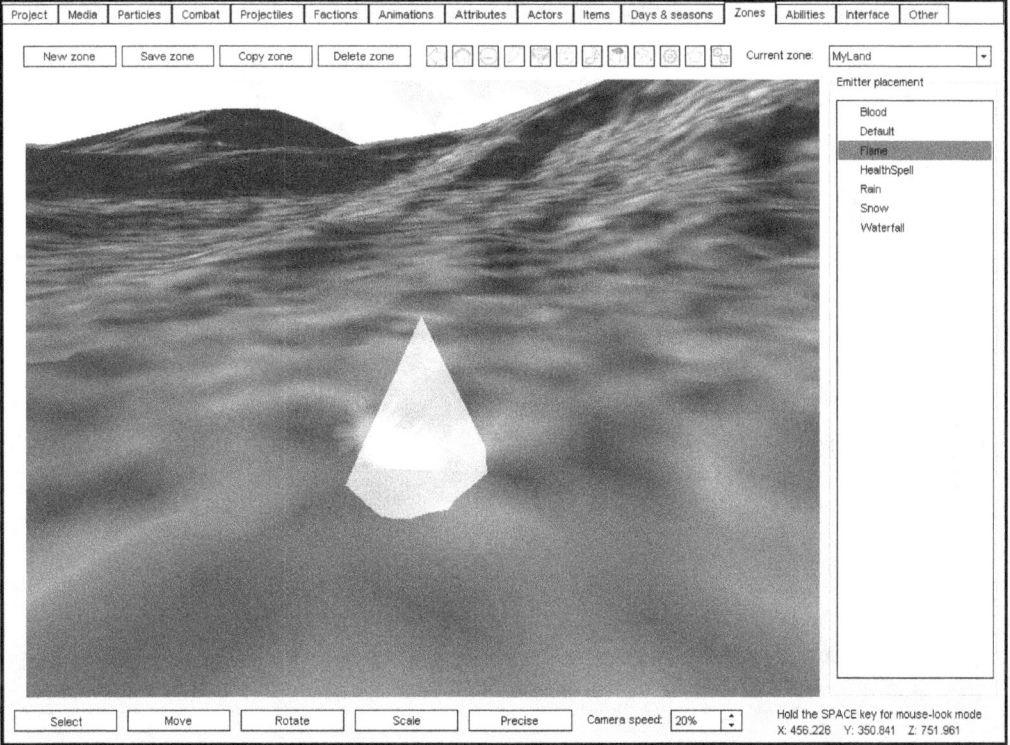

Figure 14.6 Emitters are Depicted as Cones

Emitter objects must be already created in the Emitters Tab in the Game Editor.

Emitter Placement
Placing emitters is done the same way you place other objects in the Zone Tab.

Emitter Selection List
Use this list to choose the emitter you want to place in the zone.

Emitter Options
The only option for emitters is the ability to change the particle's texture.

Change Texture
Use this drop down to select a different texture for the currently selected emitter. Through the clever use of textures, you can simulate nearly any kind of particle you can think of.

Chapter 14: Zones Tab

Water Mode

Figure 14.7 Be Sure To Scale the Water Texture Properly

Water allows for swimming and drowning.

Water can make a good barrier.

Water can be used to simulate lava, pollution, lakes, oceans, slime, fire, acid, and more.

Water Placement
Right-click the 3D View Window to place a water plane. You can drag or use Precise to adjust the size of the plane.

Water Options

Water Color
Use the RGB sliders to change the color of the water.

Change Surface Texture

Water planes have an animated water texture. Use this control to change the water surface texture.

Texture Scale

This controls the scale of the surface texture. Adjusting the scale of the surface texture helps make the water (slime, etc.) look more realistic for the size and scale of the zone it is meant to be in.

Opacity

This control is used to adjust the opacity of the water, from transparent to very murky. The opacity works along with the Water Color settings.

Damage per Second

If you want players to take damage in "water" areas, set the amount of damage per second here.

Damage Type

Use this drop down list to choose the type of damage you wish to be applied to Actors that are within the water.

Damage types are taken from the Damage Types List created in the Combat Tab.

For example, if you wanted the water to represent lava, you might set a high Damage per Second and set the Damage Type to Fire.

Another example might be corrosive acid. For that, you might choose a low Damage per Second, and set the Damage Type to Acid.

Chapter 14: Zones Tab

Collision Box Mode

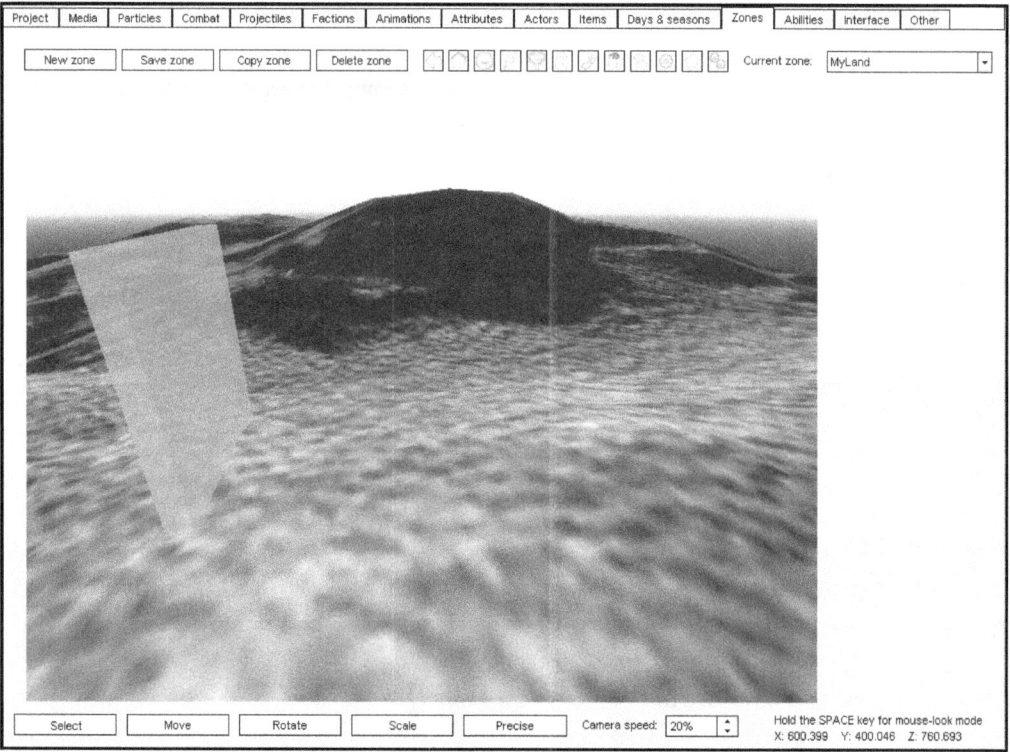

Figure 14.8 Collision Boxes Appear as Translucent Rectangles

This mode has no individual settings.

Use collision boxes to prevent players from moving into certain areas. They are, in effect, invisible walls.

Collision Box Placement
Right Click on the terrain to create a collision box.

After placing the box, use the scale, rotate, precise, and move buttons to move the collision box into place.

Sound Zone Mode

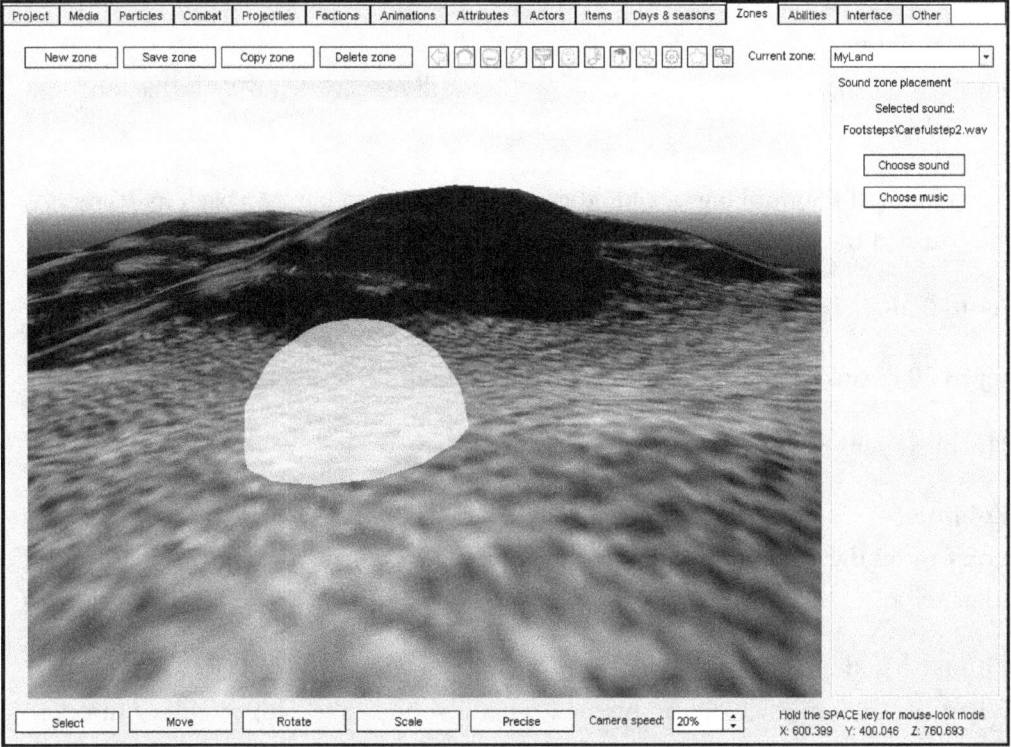

Figure 14.9 Sound Zones Appear as Yellow Spheres

Sound objects must be already loaded into the game media library via the Media Tab in the Game Editor.

3D sounds fade as the actor moves away from the center of the sound zone.

Sound Zone Placement
Place sound sounds the same way you place other objects in the Zone.

Right-click places a sound zone in the Zone Editor; the other controls (scale, move, position, etc.) are controlled normally.

Selected Sound
This is the filename of the currently selected Sound Zone.

Chapter 14: Zones Tab

Choose Sound
When selecting a sound, you can preview what it sounds like with the Play button on the selector window.

Repeat Time
This setting adjusts how long of a pause there will be between the playback of sound loops.

Keep in mind that moving outside the sound zone, then coming back in, triggers the pause in the repeat time.

Set to 0, there is no pause between the repeat of the sound loop.

Set to 30 means to pause for 30 seconds before repeating the sound loop.

The maximum repeat time pause is 1000 seconds.

Volume
You can set the volume to override the volume level the recording was made at by adjusting this control.

Choose Music
When selecting music, you can preview what it sounds like with the Play button on the selector window.

Repeat Time
This setting adjusts how long of a pause there will be between loops of the music.

Keep in mind that moving outside the music zone, then coming back in, triggers the pause in the repeat time.

Set to 0, there is no pause between the repeat of the loop.

Set to 30 means to pause for 30 seconds before repeating the music.

The maximum repeat time (pause) is 1000 seconds.

Volume
You can set the volume to override the volume level the recording was made at by adjusting this control.

A Note on Effective Audio and Sound

The proper sound effects can add great deals of ambiance to your zones, making them come alive in the mind of the player. Be careful when choosing sounds and especially music. Music should be very subtle, as it can get annoying fast.

Environmental sounds, such as birds singing, insects, buzzing, subtle wind, etc. really add a lot to make your environment more believable and immersive. Be sure your sound effects are recorded at the proper levels with respect to one another.

Use an audio editor to manipulate, amplify, and trim your sounds and music. A little work goes a long way.

Chapter 14: Zones Tab

Trigger Zone Mode

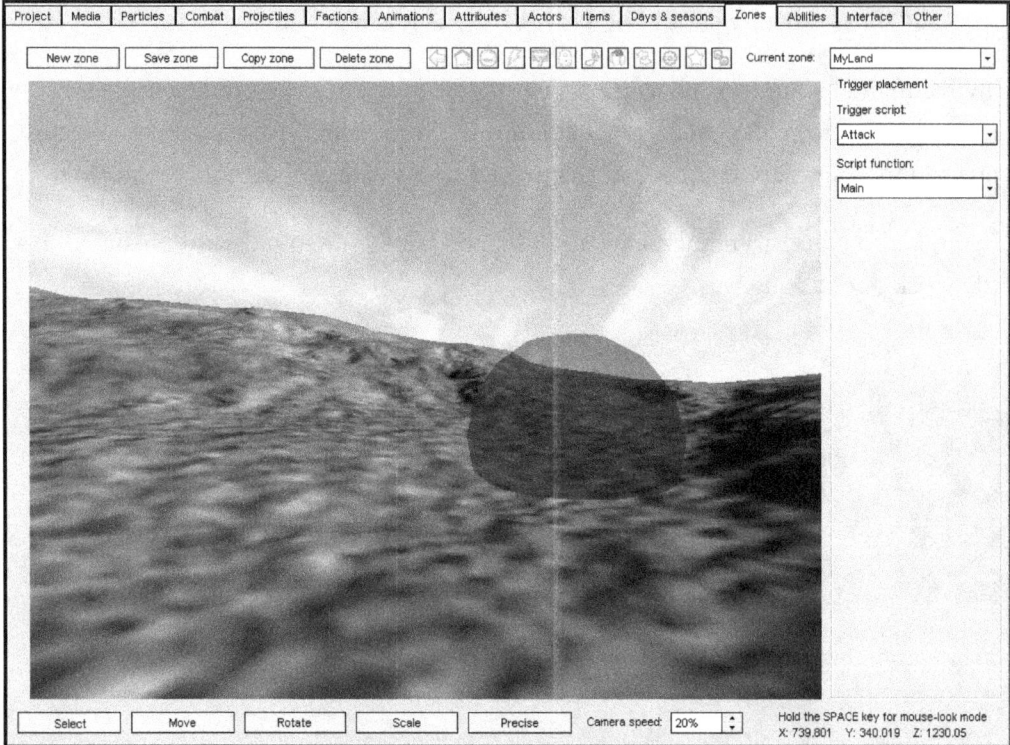

Figure 14.10 Trigger Zones Appear as Blue Spheres

Use triggers to cause scripts to run when an Actor enters the Trigger Zone.

You might use a trigger to spawn monsters when a player enters the Trigger Zone.

Another example for triggers is for setting off traps when players move into the Trigger Zone.

Trigger Placement
Place triggers by right-clicking on the terrain in the 3D View Window.

Manipulating the Trigger Zone is done the same way other objects in the zone are manipulated concerning selection, movement, scale, and so forth.

Trigger Script
Choose the script you want to trigger from the drop down list.

Keep in mind that scripts must already be written in order to be displayed on this list.

Script Function

This allows for the selection of the specific function within the chosen script that you want to run when the trigger is activated.

Selected Trigger

This area displays the attributes of the currently selected trigger.

Trigger Script

This readout displays the script that is associated with this trigger.

Script Function

This readout displays the function to be run within the chosen script.

Trigger ID

Each trigger is given a unique Trigger ID that can be used to identify the trigger in scripts.

Chapter 14: Zones Tab

Waypoint Mode

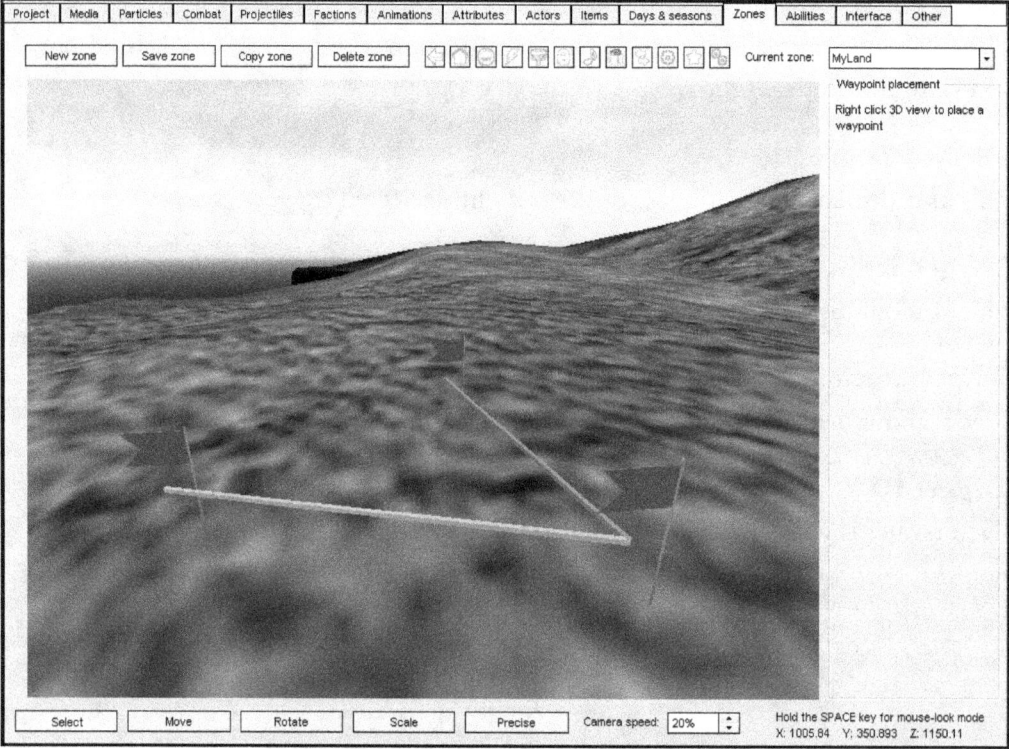

Figure 14.11 Waypoints Showing Alternate Paths;
Waypoint A Paths are Blue, B Paths are Orange

Waypoints are where Monsters and NPC's spawn (similar to Starting portals for Players).

Waypoints can be connected by paths you can set that NPC's will follow.

Use waypoints and paths to simulate patrol routes for guards, or where wolves like to roam in the forest, or any other NPC or Monster that needs to be mobile.

NPC's will follow waypoints connected by paths, pausing at each one for a designated amount of time.

When an NPC comes to a Waypoint with two path choices (path A or path B), the path to the next waypoint will be chosen randomly and the NPC will proceed to the next waypoint.

Chapter 14: Zones Tab

Waypoint Placement

Place waypoints by right-clicking in the 3D View Window. Be sure to position the marker slightly above the terrain, so the Actor doesn't fall through the ground when it is spawned.

Manipulate the position, scale, and rotation of waypoints the same way you manipulate other objects in the Zone Editor.

Waypoint Options

Set Next Waypoint A

This allows you to set a Waypoint A path from the currently selected waypoint by selecting "Set Next Waypoint A" then left-clicking on another waypoint.

No Next Waypoint A

This clears the Waypoint A from currently selected waypoint.

Set Next Waypoint B

This allows you to set a Waypoint B path from the currently selected waypoint by selecting "Set Next Waypoint B" then left-clicking on another waypoint.

No Next Waypoint B

This clears the Waypoint B from currently selected waypoint.

Pause Here For

If you want the NPC to pause at a waypoint, set the amount of time here in seconds.

Spawn This Actor Selection

Actor must have been previously defined in the Game Editor under the Actors Tab.

Spawn Script Selection

The Spawn Script must already be written and present in the appropriate script folder.

Right-click Script Selection

The Right-Click Script for this spawn must already be written and present in the appropriate script folder.

Chapter 14: Zones Tab

Death Script Selection

The Death Script for this spawn must already be written and present in the appropriate script folder.

Spawn Delay

This setting adjusts how long it takes to spawn an NPC at this waypoint.

The delay value is in seconds and the timer restarts when the currently spawned NPC/Monster is killed.

Number to Spawn

This setting adjusts how many NPC/Monsters to spawn at this waypoint.

This number is usually set to one, but can be set higher to represent swarms or rats, bugs, etc.

Auto-movement Range

If you want your NPC/Monster to be able to roam a distance from the waypoint, set that distance here.

Portal Mode

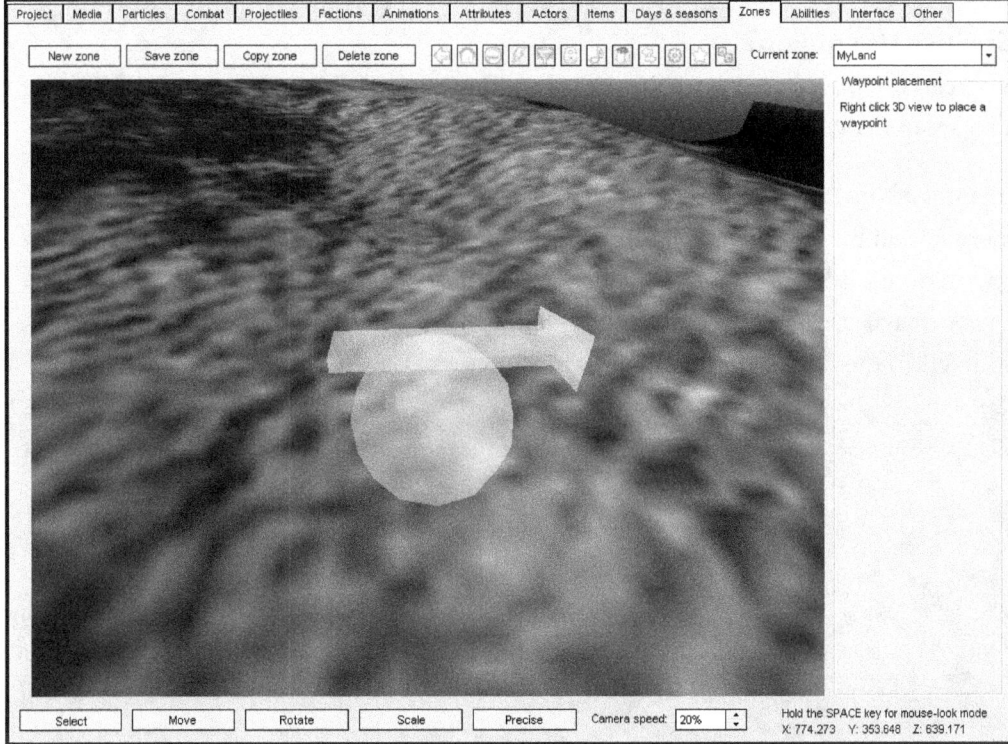

Figure 14.12 Portals Appear as Green Spheres With a Yellow Arrow Indicating the Direction the Actor Will Face When Spawning

Portals are used by PC actors to move between zones and to respawn.

Portal Placement
Place portals by right-clicking in the 3D View Window.

Use the Move and Rotate controls to be sure the portal is slightly above the ground or actors will fall through the map when they transfer through the portal.

Portal Name
Each Portal in the Zone must have a unique name within the zone.

Linked Area Selection List
If the portal links to a portal in another Zone, choose the linked Zone here.

Chapter 14: Zones Tab

Linked Portal Name Selection List

If the portal links to another portal in another Zone, use this dropdown list to choose the exact portal you wish to link to.

Creative Use of Portals

You can use portals to create graveyards where your players can respawn. You can also setup networks of portals to simulate one-way doors, mazes, or labyrinths.

Imagine if you had a prison and when your players break a law, the guards make them spawn in the prison cell until a timer is up. Remember that portals transport you between Zones. Creative use of Zones and portals will allow you to make any kind of navigation possible; from travelling across the ocean, to transporting yourself to the deck of an orbiting battleship.

Chapter 14: Zones Tab

Environment Options

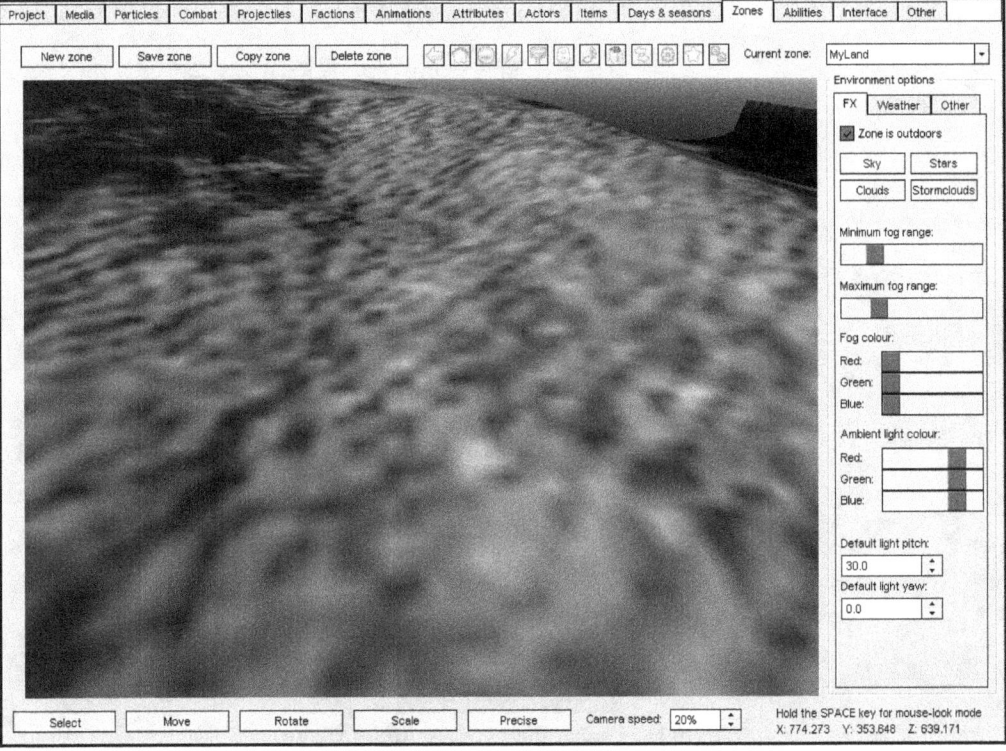

Figure 14.13 Environmental Control Panel

This is where options for the Zone environment are set.

In this section, you define what the sky looks like during the day and night, weather, fog, gravity, and more. Use these settings to customize each zone, or to make all zones act in a uniform manner.

Chapter 14: Zones Tab

FX Tab

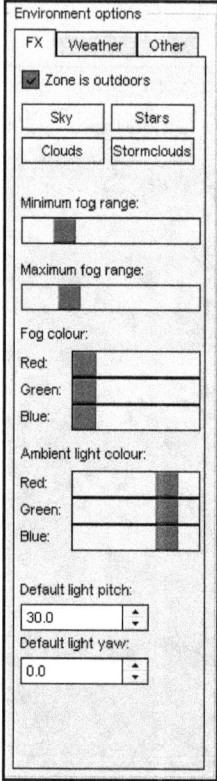

Figure 14.14 Environmental Control FX Panel

Zone is Outdoors

If the Zone is outside, check this option.

Outside Zones are flagged for use in scripts, and allow for the use of Sky, Stars, Clouds, weather, etc.

Sky

Choose the sky texture you want to use over this Zone.

Sky textures should be "spherized" for best results.

Stars

Choose the night sky texture you want to use over this Zone.

Sky textures should be "spherized" for best results.

Chapter 14: Zones Tab

Clouds
Choose the sky cloud texture you want to use over this Zone to represent cloudy conditions.

Sky textures should be "spherized" for best results.

Stormclouds
Choose the sky storm cloud texture you want to use over this Zone to simulate stormy skies.

Sky textures should be "spherized" for best results.

Minimum Fog Range
This sets how far away visual fog starts from the player camera.

Set low, the fog starts closer to the player camera.

Set high, the fogs starts farther away from the camera.

For best results, do not set the Minimum Fog Range to be greater than the Maximum Fog Range.

Maximum Fog Range
This sets how far away the visual limit is for the player camera.

Set high, there is no fog.

Set low, the fog becomes too dense to see through at shorter distances from the player camera.

Fog Color
Use the RGB sliders to set the color of the fog.

Ambient Light Color
Ambient light controls the overall lighting of the zone.

Use the RGB sliders to define the color of the ambient light across the Zone.

Default Light Pitch
This represents the position of the ambient light source along the Z Axis (north to south)

Setting of 90 places the light source directly overhead.

Setting of 0 places the light on the southern horizon.

A setting of -90 places the light source beneath the terrain.

Default Light Yaw
This represents the position of the light source around the Y Axis.

Setting of 0 places the light source in the center of the southern horizon.

Setting of 90 places the light source in the center of the eastern horizon.

Setting of 180 places the light source in the center of the northern horizon.

A setting of -90 places the light source in the center of the western horizon.

Weather Tab

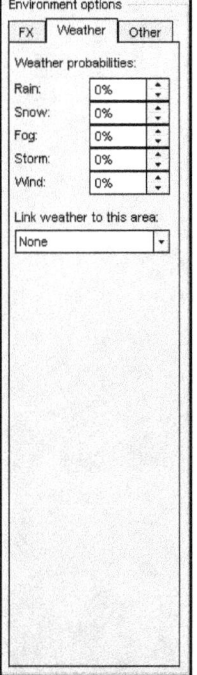

Figure 14.15 Environmental Control Weather Panel

Weather Probabilities

The probabilities of different kinds of weather occurring in this zone are controlled here.

- Rain
- Snow
- Fog
- Storm
- Wind

Link Weather to This Area

This Selection List allows the current zone to have its weather linked to the weather from another zone.

For example, if it is snowing in Zone A, it will be snowing in Zone B, if the Zones are linked.

Chapter 14: Zones Tab

Other Tab

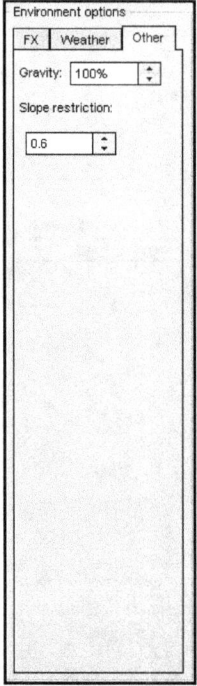

Figure 14.15 Environmental Control Other Panel

Gravity

This control adjusts the effects of gravity.

Leave this set to 100% for best results in most normal game environments.

Slope Restriction

This refers to the maximum slope an Actor can climb.

Make surfaces steep to block players from moving into certain areas.

For instance, if you put a steep mountain range around the edges of your zone, and set the Slope restriction to 50 degrees (0.5), you could keep players from climbing the "walls" of the zone and falling off the edge.

Other Options

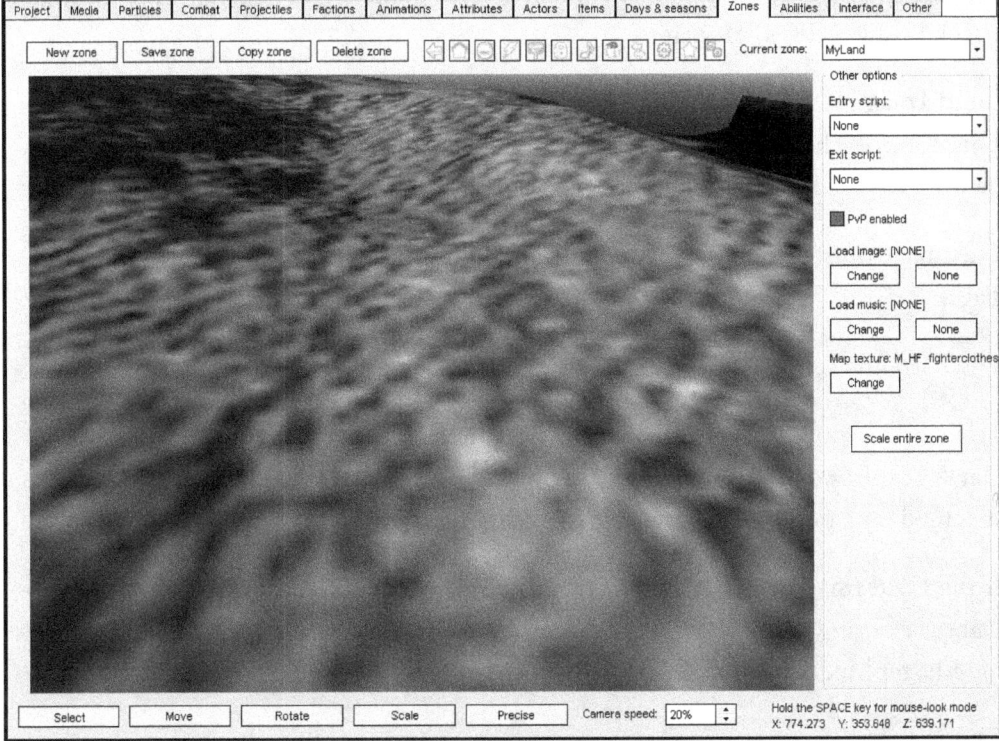

Figure 14.16 Other Options Control Panel

This section allows control over scripts that run on a player entering or leaving the zone, as well as if fighting between players is allowed, and more.

Entry Script Selection List
Use this dropdown selection list to set any script you want to run when a player enters the Zone.

The script must already exist in the script repository.

Exit Script Selection List
Use this dropdown selection list to set any script you want to run when a player leaves the Zone.

The script must already exist in the script repository.

Chapter 14: Zones Tab

PvP Enabled Option

If you want players in the Zone to be able to attack each other, check this option.

Leaving this option blank prevents players from attacking each other - they can only attack hostile NPC's/Monsters.

Load Image

This controls the image displayed while the zone is loading in the client. This can be used to give information about the zone, or game play hints.

The image must already be loaded into the Master Media List through the Media Tab.

The currently selected load image filename will be displayed.

To create random Load Images, make a folder called Random inside Data\Textures. The client will display random load screens unless otherwise specified on a per-zone basis.

If the Load Image box is empty, a random image will be used from the Data\Textures\Random folder, otherwise specify the exact image you want from the Master Media List.

Change

Use this button to change the image you want to display while the zone is loading.

None

If you don't want any load screen when entering the Zone, set it to None.

Load Music

This controls the music played while the zone is loading in the client.

The music must already exist on the Master Media List through the Media Tab.

The currently selected load music filename will be displayed.

Change

Use this button to change the Load Music.

None

If you don't want any load music for the Zone, set this to None.

MapTexture

This controls what map is displayed in the client map screen while in this zone.

The texture must already exist in the Master Media List through the Media Tab.

Scale Entire Zone

Sometimes your zone is a different size than you expected. Use this control to change the scale of the entire zone.

Chapter 15: Abilities Tab

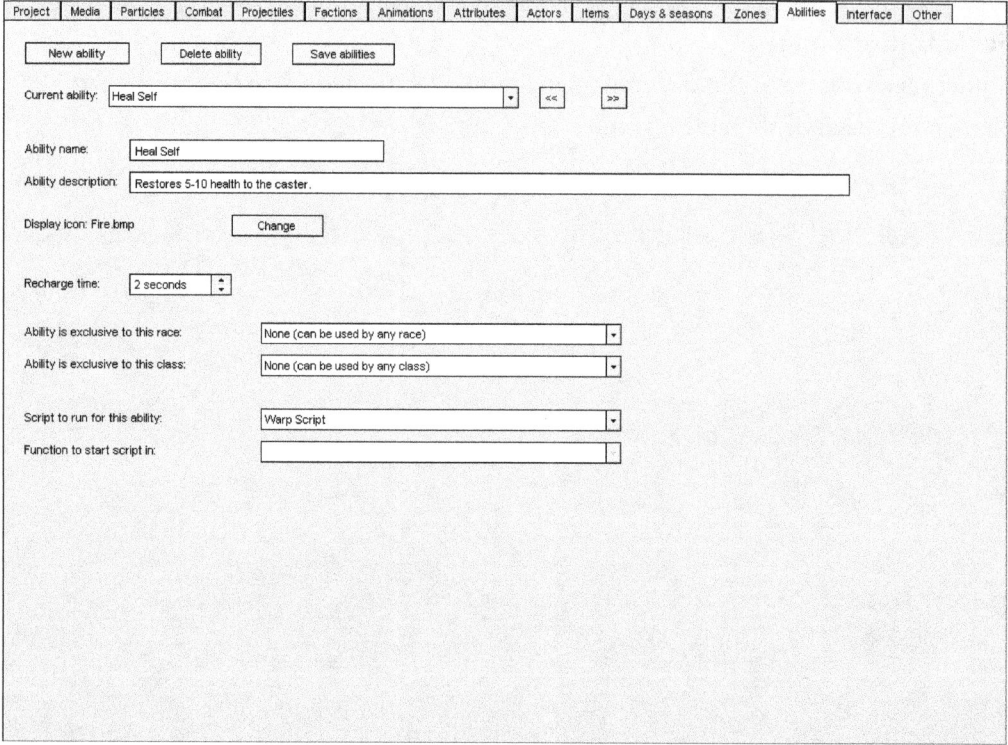

Figure 15.1 Abilities Tab

Abilities Tab Details

Abilities represent things the character can do, such as:

- **Combat maneuvers:** Such as Rend Armor, Backstab, Martial Strike, Berserk Rage, etc.
- **Magic spells:** Such as Sleep, Fireball, Mage Shield, etc.
- **Special feats:** Move Silently, Enraged, Summon Pet, Map Home, etc.

Use abilities to simulate actions common to Role Playing Games.

Abilities have associated icons, effects, and recharge times.

Abilities trigger actions through custom scripts that you define.

Chapter 15: Abilities Tab

Abilities can be set to be memorized or not memorized on the Other Tab in the Game Editor.

Managing Abilities

This area contains controls for creating, deleting, editing, and managing Abilities for your game.

New Ability

Use this button to create a new Ability.

Delete Ability

Use this button to delete the current Ability.

Save Abilities

Use this button to save the current Ability List.

Current Ability Selection List

Use this drop down selection menu to choose which Ability is currently selected.

Selection Arrows

Use the left and right arrows to move to the previous or next Ability in the Ability List.

Ability Properties

This section is for providing details about the selected ability.

Ability Name

This is the name of the currently selected Ability. You can change the name by typing over the existing name.

Ability Description

Type the Ability Description you want to be displayed in the Game Client for this Ability.

Display Icon

The currently selected icon name is listed.

Change

Use this button to change he icon for the currently selected Ability.

Chapter 15: Abilities Tab

Recharge Time

Set how long the Ability takes to recharge. The Ability cannot be activated until the recharge time has elapsed. Maximum recharge time is 60 seconds.

Ability is Exclusive to this Race Selection List

This allows the choice of "None" (any race can use this ability), or you may select the race this ability is exclusive to with the drop down selection menu.

Ability is Exclusive to this Class Selection List

This allows the choice of "None" (any Race can use this ability), or you may select the Class this ability is exclusive to with the drop down selection menu.

Script to Run for This Ability Selection List

Use this drop down selection menu to choose the script you want to run when this Ability is triggered.

Function to Start Script In Selection List

Use this drop down selection menu to choose the function you want to run when the Ability is triggered. The function must be present within the above selected script.

Chapter 16: Interface Tab

Figure 16.1 Interface Tab

Interface Tab Details

The Interface Tab allows you to design the layout of the Game Interface, as well as the Inventory Interface.

Interface Layout View

This is a preview of how the interface will look in the Game Client.

Save Interface Layout

This button saves the current Interface layout.

Game Screen / Inventory Screen Selector

Use this control to select which Interface you want to work on.

Chapter 16: Interface Tab

Interface Components List
This is a list of all the components available for the currently selected Interface. Keep in mind that although many components might be available, you are not required to place them all on the screen at once. Also, note that when an Interface Component is selected, you may not see it on the Interface Layout View. This can be because the Width and Height may be set to 0% and / or the X and Y position may be set to off-screen coordinates.

Chat Text Area Background
You may want your chat window to have a background image. This is usually discouraged because the image can interfere with the writing in the Chat Box, making the text hard to read. However, if it is set properly, you can minimize or eliminate this interference.

Change
Change the Chat Box background to a selected image. Keep in mind the image must have been previously loaded into the Media Manager.

None
Set the Chat Box to have no background image.

Component Settings
This area contains the various controls used for adjusting the currently selected Interface Component.

X Position
This control adjusts the horizontal position of the currently selected Interface Component. It controls the left / right positioning of the Interface Component. Increasing this number moves the Interface Component to the right, decreasing it moves the Interface Component to the left. The coordinates of the upper left corner of the interface are (X=0, Y=0) or just (0,0).

Y Position
This control adjusts the vertical position of the currently selected Interface Component. It controls the up / down positioning of the Interface Component. Increasing the number moves the Interface Component down the screen, decreasing the number moves the Interface Component down the screen. The coordinates of the upper left corner of the interface are (X=0, Y=0) or just (0,0).

Width
This control adjusts the width of the currently selected Interface Component.

Height
This control adjusts the height of the currently selected Interface Component.

Red
This control adjusts the amount of red used in the currently selected Interface Component. When used with the Green and Blue controls, you can set the Interface Component to whatever color you wish.

**Note: These sliders do not have numerical representations, so it is very difficult to duplicate colors.

Green
This control adjusts the amount of green used in the currently selected Interface Component. When used with the Red and Blue controls, you can set the Interface Component to whatever color you wish.

**Note: These sliders do not have numerical representations so it is very difficult to duplicate colors.

Blue
This control adjusts the amount of blue used in the currently selected Interface Component. When used with the Green and Red controls, you can set the Interface Component to whatever color you wish.

**Note: These sliders do not have numerical representations so it is very difficult to duplicate colors.

Alpha
This control adjusts the opacity of the currently selected Interface Component.

Chapter 17: Other Tab

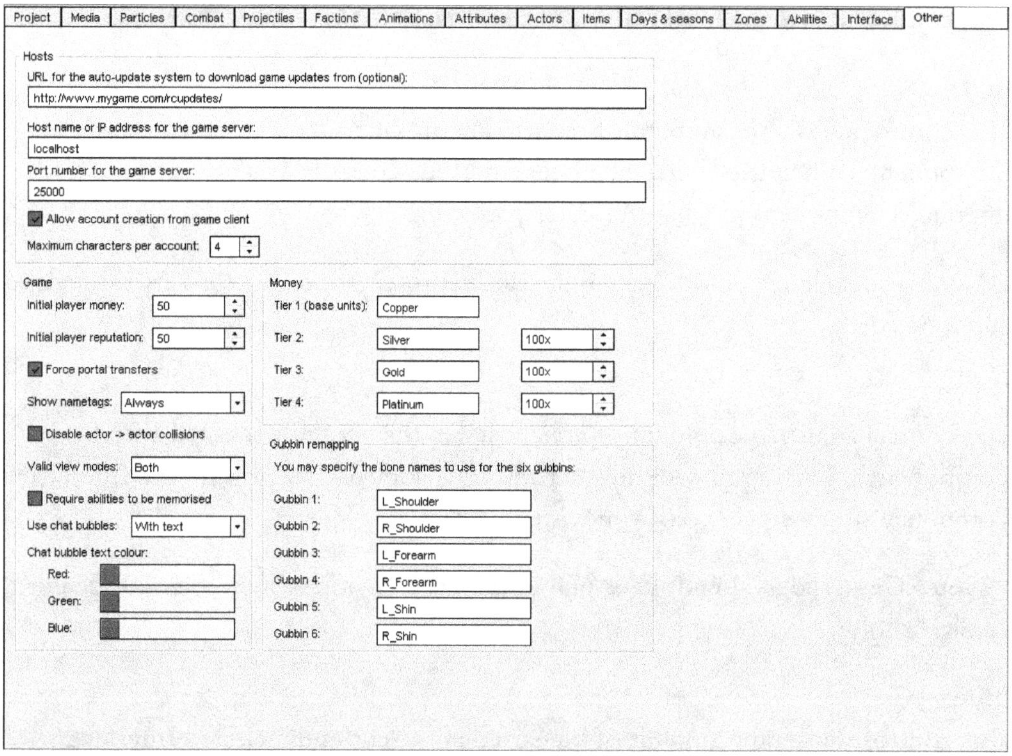

Figure 17.1 Other Tab

Other Tab Details
This area of the RCS Game Editor contains miscellaneous options for a variety of game controls and settings.

Hosts
This is the area where you setup your client and server communication information.

Host Name or IP Address for the Game Server
This field contains the IP address of the computer running the RCS Server.

When developing and testing on the same machine, use "localhost" (without quotes). The default setting for this field is localhost.

If the server is deployed to another computer on your LAN or on the Web, use the IP address of that computer. Note that if the server computer is assigned an IP address by a DHCP server, you may not get the same number you expect. It is best to manually configure the IP address of the server computer, so it cannot change.

Port Number for the Game Server
This field contains the port the RCS Server will be listening on for client connections. The default is 25000.

Allow Account Creation From the Game Client Option
This option sets whether you can create new accounts from the Game Client.

Maximum Characters per Account
This lets you set the number of characters a player can have in each account.

Maximum is 10, minimum is 1.

Game
This is where you set some options for the game. Money, reputation, nametags, and more are defined here.

Initial Player Money
Money is always given in Base Units. The default is 50 but can range from 0 to 5,000 inclusive.

Initial Player Reputation
Reputation has no default behavior in the RCS game. Use this field as a way to track "renown" or "fame". You can actually use it for any kind of thing you want to keep track of. The values can be between 0 and 5,000 inclusive.

Force Portal Transfers Option
Portals are used to move Characters from one zone to another. Use this checkbox to control whether Actors that move onto a portal are forced to transfer to the linked portal or not.

You might want to control which portals are active and which are not. One way to do this is to uncheck this option, then put a trigger where you want the players to trigger the portal from and use scripting to control the transfer of the Character.

Show Nametags
This sets whether or not Actor Nametags are shown above the actor.

- **Always-** Always show the Nametags of Actors in the Game Client.

Chapter 17: Other Tab

- **Never-** Never show Nametags in the Game Client.
- **Only on Selected-** Show Nametags only when the Actor is selected in the Game Client.

Disable Actor to Actor Collisions

If Actor Collisions are turned on, then Actors can block each other in the Game Client. This can be more realistic, but can lead to grief play.

If Actor Collisions are turned off, then Actors can pass through each other.

Valid View Modes

View Modes set which cameras will be used for the Main Screen View in the Game Editor.

- **First-** First person view is the view seen through the eyes of the Actor.
- **Third-** Third person view is the view seen from a camera floating outside the Actor, usually above and behind, facing the same direction of the Actor.
- **Both-** Selecting "Both" allows the user to freely switch between first and third person views.

Require Abilities to be Memorized Option

When this is checked, Actors must commit new abilities to their ability book before being able to use the ability. Use this as a way of simulating "learning" new abilities.

Use Chat Bubbles

This control determines whether chat bubbles are placed over the heads of Actors when engaging in chat via the Chat Window.

- **Never-** Never show chat bubbles.
- **With Text-** Chats are sent to the Chat Window, as well as the Chat Bubble.
- **Exclusively-** Chats are sent only to the Chat Bubble.

Chat Bubble Text Color

As the name implies, this controls the color of the text in the Chat Bubble. Be sure it is something that can be easily read.

Red, Green, Blue

These control the amount of red, green, and blue light used to define the color of the Chat Bubble text.

Chapter 17: Other Tab

Money

Money is any currency you might use in the game to purchase things. This can be anything from copper pieces to Imperial Star Credits. All values are with respect to the Base Unit.

Some examples:

US Currency	
Tier 1 (Base Unit): Penny	Worth 1 Penny
Tier 2: Dime	Worth 10 Pennies
Tier 3: Dollar	Worth 10 Dimes (or 100 pennies; the Base Unit)
Tier 4: Hamilton	Worth 10 Dollars (or 100 Dimes, or 1000 Pennies; the Base Unit)

Classic Adventure Currency	
Tier 1 (Base Unit): Copper	Worth 1 Copper
Tier 2: Silver	Worth 10 Copper
Tier 3: Gold	Worth 10 Silver (or 100 Copper; the Base Unit)
Tier 4: Platinum	Worth 10 Gold (or 100 Silver, or 1000 Copper; the Base Unit)

Space Opera Currency	
Tier 1 (Base Unit): Credit	Worth 1 Credit
Tier 2: KiloCredit	Worth 1000 Credits
Tier 3: MegaCredit	Worth 1000 KiloCredits (or 1,000,000 Credits; the Base Unit)
Tier 4: ImperialNote	Worth 1000 MegaCredits (or 1,000,000 KiloCredits, or 1,000,000,000 Credits; the Base Unit)

Tier 1 (Base Units) Name

This is the name of the base monetary units in your game.

Tier 2 Name

This is the name of the second denomination of currency you want to use above the Base Unit.

Tier 2 Multiplier

This is how many Base Units this Tier 2 currency will be worth.

Tier 3 Name

This is the name of the third denomination of currency you want to use above the Base Unit.

Chapter 17: Other Tab

Tier 3 Multiplier

This is how many Tier 2 units this Tier 3 currency will be worth.

Tier 4 Name

This is the name of the fourth denomination of currency you want to use above the Base Unit.

Tier 4 Multiplier

This is how many Tier 3 units this Tier 4 currency will be worth.

Gubbin Remapping

Use this if you want to change the names of the Gubbins to better suit you Actors.

Gubbin 1

Default value is L_Shoulder

Gubbin 2

Default value is R_Shoulder

Gubbin 3

Default value is L_Forearm

Gubbin 4

Default value is R_Forearm

Gubbin 5

Default value is L_Shin

Gubbin 6

Default is R_Shin

Chapter 18: RCS Game Client

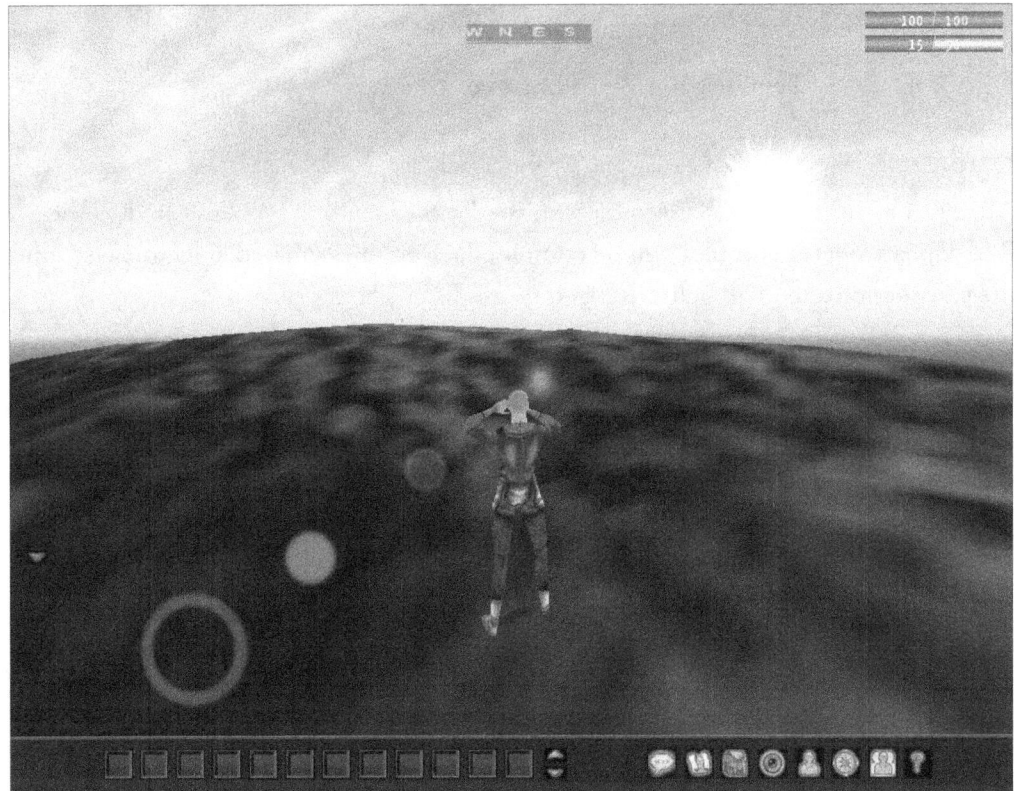

Figure 18.1 Game Client

The RCS Client is the program users run in order to connect to and interact with the virtual world contained on your Game Server. The user can create new accounts, look at their characters, create new characters, and interact with the game world.

The RCS Client contains all the interfaces, readouts, and displays needed to evaluate your status and physical position and condition in the game world. There is a backpack to hold items, a character sheet that shows your health, skills, attribute levels, a quest journal and more.

Keep in mind that all the movement, combat, and scripts are conducted on the RCS Server; the RCS client just conveys moves and displays the world status for the

Chapter 18: Game Client

player. In order to run the RCS Client, the RCS Server must be running and reachable by TCP/IP for multiplayer mode.

During development, the Author can run the RCS Test Server and RCS Test Client to preview the world and run tests.

To exit the RCS Client, use the ESC key twice.

Updates

After logging into the RCS Game server, the RCS Client will be connected to the RCS Update Server and files will be compared. New files created since the last time the Client connected will be transferred to the RCS Client.

Updates are best kept on a different server from the Game Server. When Clients login to the Server, updates are transferred to the Client. If the Game Server and the Update Server were the same computer, there would be performance hits every time a new, un-updated client logged in, hogging up the bandwidth used for the game.

Chapter 18: Game Client

Client Details

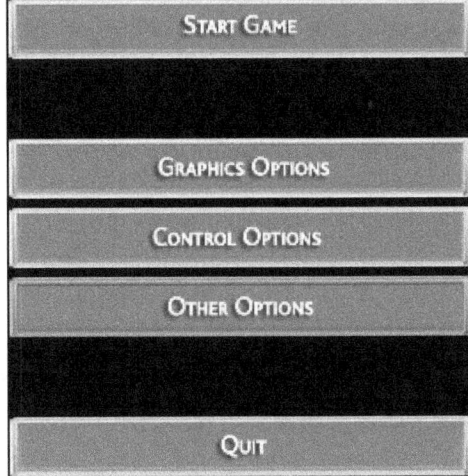

Figure 18.2 Client Main Menu

Start Game
Clicking the Start Game button launches the client Account Login window.

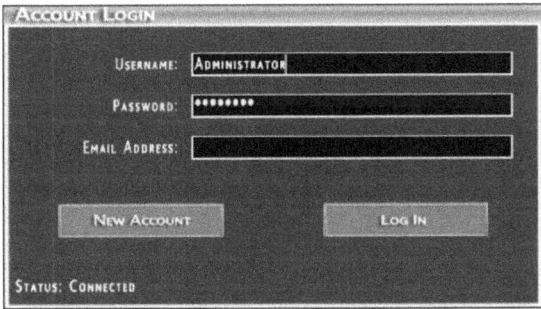

Figure 18.3 Client Account Login Window

This window is where the player can enter their account information and login to the Game Server (Game Server must be running and accessible).

Username
This field takes the player's Username. Usernames must be unique. Think of Usernames as accounts. Keep in mind this is to identify the player; characters you create in the Game Client have their own names.

Password
This field takes the password associated with the player's Username.

Chapter 18: Game Client

Email Address

This field is required only when creating a new account. There are different ways to manage accounts. One way is to allow users to self-register. Another way is to have them register through some kind of third-party management system. Currently the Client is setup for self-registration.

New Account

If you want to create a new User Account, click this button after filling in Username, Password, and Email fields (see above).

Authors can disable the ability of users to create new accounts. In that case, the author is responsible for creating an Account Management System.

Login

If you have already created an account, click this button to login to the Client after filling out the Username and Password fields.

Graphics Options

This screen contains various controls to configure and optimize the client for a variety of graphics cards and personal preferences.

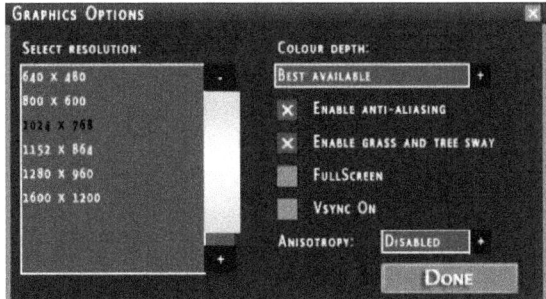

Figure 18.4 Client Graphics Options Window

Select Resolution

This allows the user to set the desired resolution of the client.

Color Depth

This sets the number of bits used to render the graphics.

- 16 - 4096 colors
- 32- 16 million colors
- Best Available

Enable Anti-aliasing

Check this box to make graphics look smoother along the edges.

Enable Grass and Tree Sway

Trees and grass can be set to sway in the wind. If you have a good video card, you can enable this feature. Keep in mind that this only works with grass and trees made with the RC Tree Editor.

Fullscreen

The client can run in Windowed and Full-screen modes. Use this checkbox to enable Full-screen mode.

Vsync On

Vsync reduces visual tearing that may occur on low-end video cards. Set this to ON in order to make screen updates during the vertical refresh of your monitor.

Chapter 18: Game Client

Anisotropy

This controls the level of image enhancement applied to textures viewed at oblique angles. The higher the number, the clearer the graphics are on distant objects viewed at oblique angles.

- x4
- x8
- x16
- Disabled

Done

This button saves the settings and closes the Graphics Options window, returning the user to the Main Menu.

Control Options

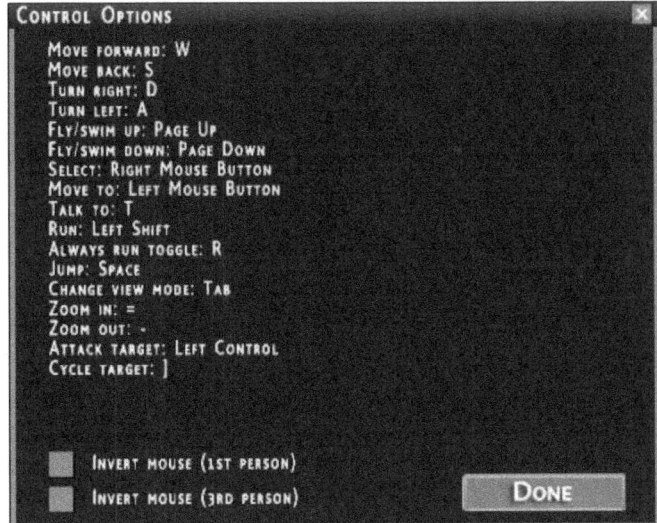

Figure 18.5 Client Control Options Window

Control List

This is a list of all the game controls.

If you want to change what keys are bound to the controls, just click the control and select the new key to associate it with.

Invert Mouse - 1st Person

This flips the vertical axis of the mouse when in 1st Person view. Inverted mouse controls are used to simulate flying games, where pulling back (moving the mouse down) spins the camera back therefore making the view look up. Likewise, pushing the mouse forward would tip the camera forward, therefore looking down.

Invert Mouse - 3rd Person

This flips the vertical axis of the mouse when in 3rd Person view. Inverted mouse controls are used to simulate flying games, where pulling back (moving the mouse down) spins the camera back therefore making the view look up. Likewise, pushing the mouse forward would tip the camera forward, therefore looking down.

Done

This button saves the settings and closes the Control Options window, returning the user to the Main Menu.

Chapter 18: Game Client

Other Options

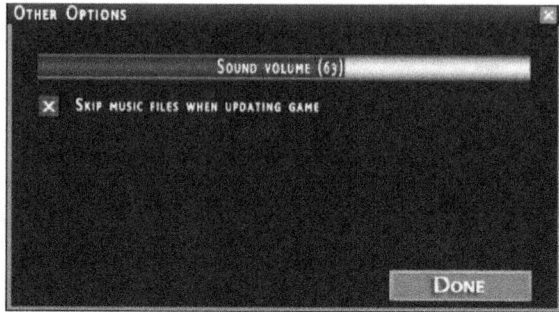

Figure 18.6 Client Other Options Window

Sound Volume
Set the volume level between 0 and 100 percent with the slider control.

Skip Music Files While Updating Game
Check this box to have the client skip over music files when updating. This can make the updates go faster, but deprives the user of certain audio files.

Done
This button saves the settings and closes the Other Options window, returning the user to the Main Menu.

Character Selection Screen

The Character Selection Screen is where the player creates new characters, deletes old characters, or chooses one of her existing characters to play.

If a character already exists for this Username, they will be listed in the panel on the left.

The Character selection background is a 3D set defined in the following location: \Realm Crafter 1\Projects\New Project\Data\Meshes\Character Set\Set.b3d

New Character
New characters can be created using the New Character button. The Player will be taken to another screen where she can define the starting Statistics for her new character.

Chapter 18: Game Client

<< and >>

These buttons rotate the camera view so you can look at all sides of your currently selected character.

Delete Character

Old characters, or characters that you don't want to use, can be deleted using the Delete Character button. Be careful when using this button, as deleted characters and all their gear are destroyed forever.

Start Game

Use the Start Game button to launch the Game Client with the currently selected character.

Chapter 18: Game Client

Creating a New Character

Figure 18.7 Client Character Creation

The Character Creation Screen allows the player to create new characters to play in the game world. There are various controls to change different aspects of the character. By changing hair, clothes, and gender players can customize their character's appearance.

Character Window

Race- Select the character's Race. All playable races will be listed here. Races are defined and set for "playable" from the RCS Game Editor. Changing this setting also changes the Race Description located below the window.

Gender- Select the character's Gender (usually male and female). Different hair and clothes options are available for the two genders. Genders are setup in the RC Game Editor.

144

Class- Select the character's Class here. Think of a character's Class as her profession. Class options are created in the RC Game Editor.

Hair- Use this to select the character's hair style. Available hair models are defined in the RC Game Editor.

Face- Use this control to select different head models available for the selected Race. Head models are loaded and defined in the RC Game Editor.

Beard- This allows the player to select different beard models. Beards are defined in the RC Game Editor.

Clothes- This allows the player to select different sets of starting clothes. Clothes are defined in the RC Game Editor.

Attributes Window

This window allows the player to change the starting values of various Attributes. If the Author has allowed extra points to spend on Attributes, the amount left will be displayed here as well. Spendable Attribute Points are defined in the RC Game Editor.

Name Window

Type in the name you want for your character. The RC Server will search through the existing character database to be sure the name has not already been taken.

Authors can restrict user names by using the name filter file located at:

<projectName>\Data\Server Data\Names Filter.txt

Chapter 18: Game Client

Game Client Main Screen

Figure 18.8 Game Client Main Screen

The main screen is where the user interacts with the game.

Compass
The compass is optional and indicates which direction the player is facing.

Chat Window
This is where messages from the game, as well as other players, are displayed.

Status Bars
It is common to display some Status Bars, such as Life and Mana, to help the player know their disposition in the game.

Chapter 18: Game Client

Game Toolbar

Figure 18.9 Game Client Toolbar

Action Bar- There are twelve Quick Slots available. Place Abilities on the Action Bar to trigger them on-demand. Available Abilities are located in the Abilities screen. There are 3 Action Bars to choose from. Use the arrow buttons to select the Action Bar you want. This allows you to setup one Action Bar for combat, another for crafting, and the third for any custom purpose of your choice.

Game Toolbar Icons:

Chat	**Chat** This button opens up a command line that can be used to chat with other players or to type in commands.
Map	**Map** This button opens up a Zone Map Window. Zone Maps are defined on a Zone-by-Zone basis in the Game Editor.
Inventory	**Inventory** This button opens up the Character's backpack and allows the player to outfit armor, weapons, and gear.
Abilities	**Abilities** This opens up the Abilities Window, allowing access to Ability Icons that can be placed on the Action Bar for quick activation.
Character	**Character** This opens up the Character Window, which lists information on the current state of the Character and her Attributes.
Quest	**Quest Journal** This opens up the Quest Journal Window, which displays the status of all current Quests.
Party	**Party** This window lists all party members and allows the player to leave the party or to send messages to other members of the party.
Help	**Help** This displays an in-game help screen in a scrollable window. The contents of this window can be editing using the file located here:

Chapter 18: Game Client

Inventory

Figure 18.10 Client Inventory Window

The top row provides slots for weapon, shield, helmet, chest, gloves, belt, legs, and shoes. The next row allows the character to wear 4 rings and 2 amulets. The next section is the contents of the character's inventory. There are 32 slots that can hold items in the Inventory window.

To pick up an item, click on it, move it to where you want to place it, and click again. If you are not sure where something belongs, pick it up then click on the USE button. Money is listed at the bottom. If you want to drop an item, click to select it, and then click the DROP button.

Chapter 18: Game Client

Abilities

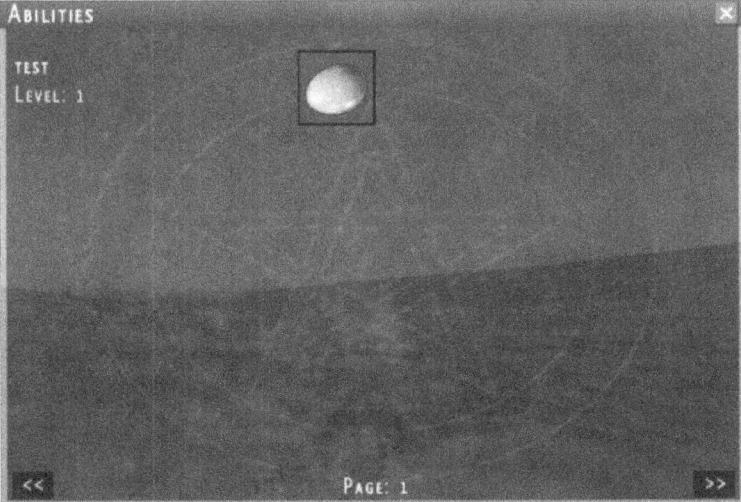

Figure 18.11 Game Client Abilities Window

Abilities are used for special combat maneuvers, casting spells, etc. Drag Abilities to the Quickslots on the Action Bars to trigger them easily.

Chapter 18: Game Client

Character Sheet

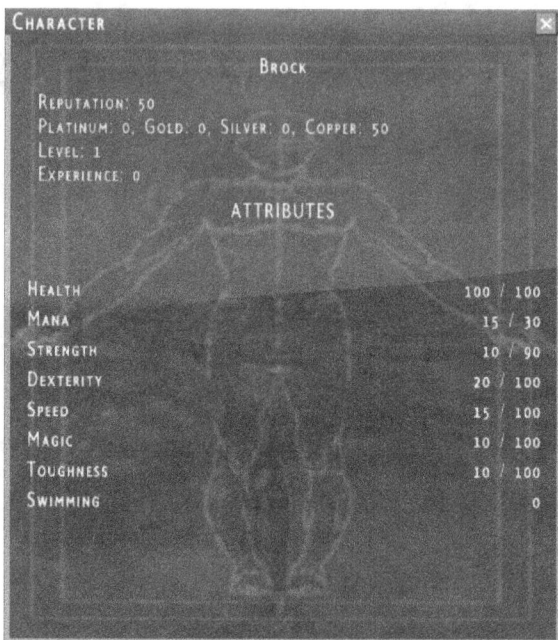

Figure 18.12 Game Client Character Window

The Character Sheet displays all the details about your Character including your Level, Money, and Characteristics.

Chapter 18: Game Client

Quest Journal

Figure 18.13 Game Client Quests Window

The Quest Journal displays the current status of all Quests accepted by the player.

A checkbox toggles the display of completed quests.

Quests are programmed using custom scripts. Scripting is beyond the scope of this book, but will be covered in another publication.

I have included a sample quest script for a Talk Quest. The player must talk to the Patron to start the quest. The player is instructed to talk to a Guard called Merok. When the player chats with Merok with a right-click, the player gets a dialog from Merok and is rewarded 10 coins and 5 XP. Any interaction with the Patron after the quest is complete will give a "thank you" message.

Open up a text editor and save myQuest.rsl in the following folder:
<projectName>\Data\Server Data\Scripts

Chapter 18: Game Client

Sample Quest Script

Listing 18.1   `myQuest.rsl` - **A simple talk quest**

```
Using "RC_Core.rcm"

Function Main()
; talk quest
; set quest as persistent to survive crashes and logouts
Persistent(1)

; get player's id
player% = Actor()

; get NPC ID
target% = ContextActor()

; get NPC name
targetName$ = Name(target)

; wait to speak with an  NPC
waitSpeakName$ = "Guard Merok"

; set questName
questName$ = "Find Guard Merok"

; quest status will be empty if the quest has not started
questResults$ = QuestStatus(player, questName)

; set msg to hold messages but for now it is blank
msg$ = ""

; check to see if the quest has been completed
if questResults <> ""
    ; quest has already been completed
    ; send thank you message
    d% = OpenDialog(player, target, targetName)

    ; set message text
    msg = "Thanks for finding " + waitSpeakName + "."

    DialogOutput(player, d, msg, 255, 255, 128)

    ; pause for a second and half then close the dialog
    DoEvents(1500)
    closeDialog(player, d)

else
    ; quest has not been accepted

    ; setup temp variable for dialog results
    result% =0
```

```
; get player
playerName$ = Name(player)

; get the id number of the NPC
waitSpeakID% = FindActor(waitSpeakName, 2)

; exchange greetings with player
; open a dialog box and get a dialog window handle id
d% = OpenDialog(player%, target%, targetName$)

; Player greets NPC
; setup output message
msg = "Hail " + targetName + "!"

DialogOutput(player, d, msg, 0, 128, 255)

; pause for 1 second
DoEvents (1000)

; NPC greets player
; setup output message
msg = "Hail " + playerName + "!"
DialogOutput(player, d, msg, 255, 255, 128)

; pause for 1 second
DoEvents (1000)

; display the proposed quest objective
msg = "Please find " + waitSpeakName + "."
DialogOutput(player, d, msg, 255, 255, 128)

; get user choice
msg = "It will be an honor!|No sorry I am too busy"
result% = DialogInput(player, d, msg, "|")

; player chooses the first option start the new quest
If (result% = 1)
    ; set quest objective text - chr(44) is a comma
    msg = "Find " + waitSpeakName + CHR(44)
    msg = msg + " he was last seen leaving the guard tower "
    msg = msg + "for his usual patrol."

    questStatusText$ = msg
    ; Create the new quest
    ; define a new quest sends a chat message of 'quest Log Updated'
    NewQuest(player, questName, questStatusText, 241, 227, 126)

    ; send a status message to the chat window
    questMsg$ = questName + ": " + questStatusText
    Output(player, questMsg, 255, 255, 255)

    ; Close the dialog box
```

Chapter 18: Game Client

```
        CloseDialog(Player, d)

        ; program pauses here until npc is right clicked
        WaitSpeak(player, waitSpeakID)
        ; NPC has been right clicked by player
        ; talk to NPC
        d = OpenDialog(player, waitSpeakID, waitSpeakName)

        ; set the quest to completed status
        CompleteQuest(player, questName)

        ; Money reward for Step/Quest
        ChangeGold(player, 10)

        ; XP reward for Step/Quest
        GiveXp(player, 5)

        msg = "You earn 10 coins and 5 XP for finding "
        msg = msg + WaitSpeakName + "!"
        Output(player,msg)

        ; note targetname is the npc that gave the quest
        msg = "So " + targetName + " sent you to find me?"
        DialogOutput(player, d, msg, 255, 255, 128)

        DialogResult = DialogInput(player, d, "Goodbye")

        closeDialog(player, d)

    Else
        ; player declined quest so just close the dialog
        CloseDialog(player, d)

    EndIf

EndIf

End Function
```

Now that the quest has been defined, we need to create another actor for the player to interact with to complete the quest. We want that actor to set its name to Guard Merok. This is done through the Spawn Script selector on a Waypoint.

Open up a text editor and save `Merok-init.rsl` in the following folder:
<projectName>\Data\Server Data\Scripts

Chapter 18: Game Client

Listing 18.2   `Merok-init.rsl` - **Assigning a Name to an Actor**

```
Using "RC_Core.rcm"

Function Main()
    ; set the name of the NPC
    Name$ = "Guard Merok"

    ; get the handle for this actor
    NPC% = Actor()

    ; set the actor's name
    SetName(NPC, Name)
End Function
```

Go to the Zone Tab and place a waypoint on the terrain where you want the NPC to spawn. In the Waypoint Options, under Spawn this Actor, select another stock Human Fighter.

Now we want to assign a right-click script to the Human Fighter, so in the Waypoint Options, under Spawn Script, choose the `Merok-init.rsl` script.

Be sure to use the Precise placement controls to move the waypoint flag marker above the terrain somewhat, otherwise the spawned actor's feet will be below the terrain and it will fall through.

You are now ready to test your script. Start up the Test Server and Test Client, and then go to the Quest Patron and right-click to interact. You should be given the option to take the quest. After you have selected the quest, find Guard Merok and right-click him to complete the quest.

If your quest does not seem to be working, shut down the test server and check the error logs. Script failure is normally because of typos in the script.

Chapter 18: Game Client

Controlling the Game

Moving

You can steer your character using the normal WASD controls commonly used in first-person games.

You can also click a place on the terrain and the Character will move in a straight line towards that point.

The graphic for the Movement Marker is located at:
\Realm Crafter 1\Projects\New Project\Data\Textures\GUI\PartyBG.bmp

Trading

In order to trade with other players, select the player you want to trade with and type /trade. If the other player wants to trade, they type /accept and a Trade Window will open.

Forming a Party

To form a party with other players, type: /invite PlayerName

To leave the party, type: /leave.

In-game Commands

Certain commands can be entered directly into the Chat. All in-game commands are preceded with the slash character "/".

There are many built-in commands, and Authors can add additional commands through scripting via the In-game Commands.rsl file.

GM Commands

There are several commands that are useful to the GM. Player GM status is set in the RC Server in the Account Window.

/ability <abilityName>, <level>
Sets the indicated GM's Ability to the level requested.
Example: /ability heal self, 10

/give <itemName>
Places the indicated item into the GM's inventory.
Example: /give sword

/gm <message>
Sends a message to all GM's that are logged on.
Example: /gm Hello other GM's!

/gold <amount>
Puts an amount of base currency into the GM's inventory.
Example: /gold 10

/kick <characterName>
This command kicks a player off the server, disconnecting their client. Player can rejoin game.
Example: /kick joe

/script <scriptName>, < functionName>
Runs the function in the indicated script.
Example: /script myScript, crafting

/setAttribute <attributeName>, <value>
This command sets the value of the Attribute to the amount indicated.
Example: /setattribute mana, 20

Chapter 18: Game Client

/setAttributeMax <attributeName>, <value>
This sets the maximum value of an Attribute to the value indicated.
Example: /setattributemax mana, 77

/warp <zoneName>
Teleports the GM to the Start Portal of the Zone indicated.
Example: /warp myZone

/weather <weatherType>
This sets the weather for the Zone the GM is currently in. Valid weather types are: sun, sunny, normal, rain, rainy, snow, snowy, rain, rainy, fog, foggy, wind, windy, storm, stormy, thunder, lightning.
Example: /weather rain

/warpother <characterName>, <zonename>
This command teleports (warps) a player to the Start Portal of any zone. Works on any character currently logged in. Character does not have to be in the same zone as the GM that gives this command.
Example: /warpother joe, swamplands

/xp <amount>
This adds the indicated number of XP points to the GM's character.
Example: /xp 100

Player Commands:
Player commands are available to help players for groups, trade, control their pets, and more.

/allPlayers
This displays how many other players are currently logged onto the server.
Example: /allplayers

/ignore <characterName>
This command is used to prevent other characters from chatting with you.
Example: /ignore joe

/unignore <characterName>
This command is used to remove other characters from your Ignore List.
Example: /unignore joe

Chapter 18: Game Client

/date
This command displays the current in-game date.
Example: /date

/g <message>
This sends a message to all the players in your group. Group is different than Party. Group is meant to simulate Guilds and is defined through scripting.
Example: /g hello guild!

/invite <playerName>
This invites another player to join your party. The invited player must type /accept. Maximum group size is 7.
Example: /invite joe

/leave
This quits the current party (bug: leaves member on the party list after they quit).
Example: /leave

/me <message>
This displays an 'emote' message. Other players see "playerName <message>".
Example: /me dances a jig!

/p <message>
This sends a message to all the members of your party.
Example: /p Let's get out of here!

/pet <petName>, <petCommand>
Pet Name can be any pet's name or the word "all".
Valid pet commands are: stay, wait, come, follow, attack, "name, <newName>"
Example: /pet fido, stay
Example: /pet fido, name, spot
Example: /pet all, attack

/players
This display the number of other players in the current zone.
Example: /players

/pm <playerName>, <message>
This sends a private message to another player. Target player must be logged-in.
Example: /pm joe, meet me at the tavern

159

Chapter 18: Game Client

/season

Displays the current season in the game world. Seasons are defined by the Author in the RC Game Editor.

Example: /season

/time

This command displays the current in-game time.

Example: /time

/trade <playerName>

Sends a trade request to another player. Other player must respond with /accept to activate the Trade Window.

Example: /trade joe

/yell <message>

Sends a message across all zones on the server.

Example: /yell I need help!

Chapter 19: Customizing the Client

The Client can be customized by editing certain graphics files, also called "re-skinning". This process gives your game a certain "look and feel" which is unique to your project.

You can also customize the client by editing the language file.

Localizing and Customizing the Client Language

If you want to deploy your game client in different languages, or change the default labels and prompts, you can edit the output language of the Game Client interface, as well as the Game Client Updater.

Updater Language File

This is an important file not only because of the customization it offers, but it also helps configure the RC Updater (see Chapter 20).

Located at:

\projects\language.txt

Misspelled "Finnished"

RC Game Client Language file

Located at:

\projects\<projectName>\Data\Game Data\Language.txt

Customizing the Action Bar

It is possible to customize the action bar with your own graphics.

The Action Bar area consists of space for the Quick Slots, the Game Toolbar, the XP Meter, and the Chat/Command Prompt.

The Action Bar file is 1024x128 and located here:
\projects\<projectName>\Data\Textures\GUI\Action Bar.bmp

Chapter 19: Customizing The Client

Customizing the Client Layer
The main screen can have an underlying Client Layer that can be used for borders, decoration, or stylized treatment.

The image should be 1024x768 and can be masked or have an alpha channel. By default, black areas are transparent. If you want to make something like black use RGB 0, 0, 1 to simulate black without the transparent mask.

The default Client Layer can be found here:
\projects\<projectName>\Data\Textures\GUI\Action Bar_full.dds

If that is not found, the Client loads the following:
\projects\<projectName>\Data\Textures\GUI\Action Bar_full.bmp

Customizing the Compass
The compass graphic can be changed by customizing the following graphics files:

- <projectName>\Data\Textures\Compass.PNG
- <projectName>\Data\Textures\Compass Overlay.PNG

The compass can be moved around using the Interface Tab of the RC Game Editor.

Customizing the Status Bars
The position and color of the bars can be changed in the RC Game Editor under the Interface Tab.

Customizing the Inventory Window
The Inventory icon is located at:
Realm Crafter 1\Projects\New Project\Data\Textures\GUI\Inventory.bmp

The Inventory background is located at:
\Realm Crafter 1\Projects\New Project\Data\Textures\GUI\InventoryBG.bmp

Customizing the Abilities Window
The Abilities icon is located at:
Realm Crafter 1\Projects\New Project\Data\Textures\GUI\Abilities.bmp

The background for the Abilities window is located at:
\Realm Crafter 1\Projects\New Project\Data\Textures\GUI\AbilitiesBG.bmp

Chapter 19: Customizing The Client

Customizing the Character Window
The Character icon is located at:
Realm Crafter 1\Projects\New Project\Data\Textures\GUI\Character.bmp

The background for the Character window is located at:
\Realm Crafter 1\Projects\New Project\Data\Textures\GUI\CharBG.bmp

Customizing the Quest Journal Window
The Quest Journal icon is located at:
Realm Crafter 1\Projects\New Project\Data\Textures\GUI\Quests.bmp

The background for the Quest Journal Window is located at:
\Realm Crafter 1\Projects\New Project\Data\Textures\GUI\QuestLogBG.bmp

Customizing the Party Window
The Party icon is located at:
\Realm Crafter 1\Projects\New Project\Data\Textures\GUI\Party.bmp

The background for the Party Window is located at:
\Realm Crafter 1\Projects\New Project\Data\Textures\GUI\PartyBG.bmp

Customizing the Help Window
The Help icon is located at:
\Realm Crafter 1\Projects\New Project\Data\Textures\GUI\Help.bmp

The background for the Help Window is located at:
\Realm Crafter 1\Projects\New Project\Data\Textures\GUI\HelpBG.bmp

You can change the contents of the Help window for this individual game client by editing the Help file located at:
\Realm Crafter1\Projects\<projectName>\Data\Help.txt

You can change the master Help template at:
\Realm Crafter1\Data\Default Project\Data\Help.txt

Chapter 20: The Game Server

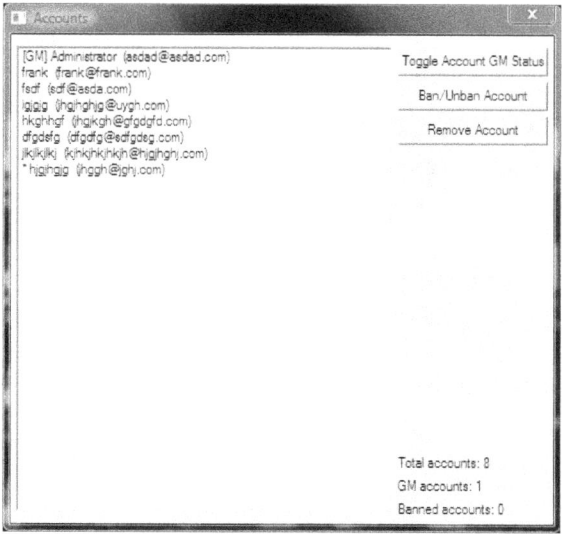

Figure 20.1 Server Accounts Window

The RC Server program controls the Client connections to the Game World and coordinates the interaction between Players on different Clients. In order to host a game you must run the Game Server on a computer then access the Game Server over a network using a Game Client.

The RC Game Server receives input from the Game Clients then runs scripts and makes calculations based on that input. The results of those calculations, including positions of all the buildings, the players, the monsters, shops, and treasures in the Game World are then sent back to the Client, which renders the scene for the Player.

Any time you make changes to scripts, you should update and deploy a new Game Serer, as the scripts are handled by the Game Server.

Any time you make changes to the content of your Game World, you should deploy a new Game Client, as well as provide patches to update existing Game Client installations.

Server Accounts Window

This window allows management and certain administrative control over the Player Accounts registered with the Server.

Account List

This window displays all the players with accounts on the Server.

When a player is connected, the Server will display an asterisk '*' next to that player's name on the list.

The Account List also displays a player's GM status by displaying '[GM]' next to the player's name on the list.

Accounts can be selected by clicking them with the mouse. When an Account is selected, different options can be applied to it.

Toggle Account GM Status

Players with GM status have access to Administrative level functions, such as granting XP, creating items directly in their inventory, and more. See the section of the RC Client regarding GM Commands.

To toggle a Player's GM status, select the Account and click this button.

Ban/Unban Account

If a player is causing trouble on your Server, you can Ban the Account. Banned Players are prevented from logging into the Game World.

To toggle a Ban, select the Account and click the Ban button.

Remove Account

When Accounts become banned or unused, Administrators can delete them.

To Remove an Account, select the Account and click the Remove Account button.

Chapter 20: The Game Server

Server Game Status Window

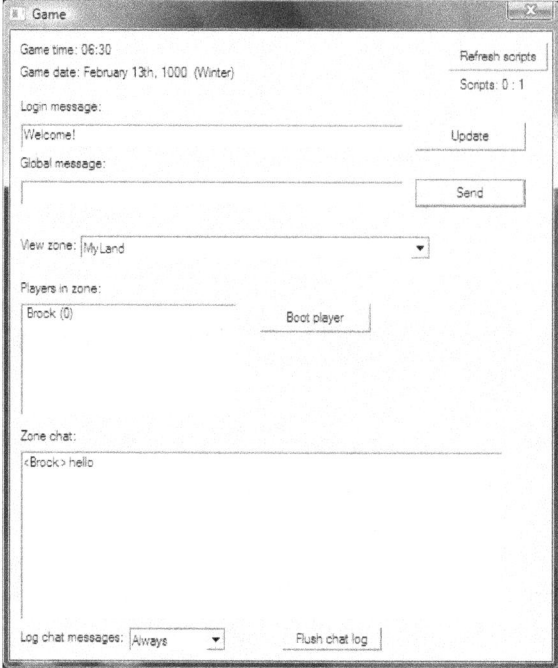

Figure 20.2 Server Game Status Window

This window provides the Administrator with ongoing information about the status of the currently running Game Server.

Game Date and Time
This display contains the current game Time and Date, along with the current Season. Timescale and seasons are defined by the Author in the RC Game Editor.

Refresh Scripts
If you make edits to any scripts, you can bring those online by using the Refresh Scripts button. This is very useful for troubleshooting, or implementing a quick fix to something without having to bring down the server. Think of this as a Live Update for the scripts on the Server.

Below the Refresh Scripts button, there is a Scripts Display containing the number of active scripts, and the number of looping scripts.

Login Message
Enter a message to be displayed when players login to the game, then press the Update button to set the Login Message.

Example Login Messages:

- Welcome! Have fun!
- Don't forget the tournament coming up this weekend!

Global Message

When the Administrator wants to send out server-wide messages, they can be entered into the Global Message field and sent with the Send button.

Example Global Messages:

- Server going down for maintenance in 10 minutes!
- The armies of darkness are attacking the castle!

View Zone

The Administrator can monitor specific Zones by selecting them from this list.

Players in Zone

This area displays a roster of all the players in the selected zone.

Boot Player

If a player is causing trouble, the Administrator can boot the player from the server. Booting the player immediately disconnects them from the server.

To boot a player, select them on the Players in Zone list and then click the Boot Player button.

Zone Chat

This window displays a running log of every chat sent in the zone. This can be used to monitor player interactions.

Log Chat Messages

This controls how Chat Logs are created. The Chat Log can be read with any standard text editor.

Chapter 20: The Game Server

The Chat Log can be found here:
<projectName>\Data\Logs\Chat Log.txt

- **Always**- Log all chat messages in all zones.
- **Never**- Do not log messages.
- **This Zone Only**- Logs all chat messages in the selected zone.
- **Flush Chat Log**- Clears out the chat log.

Server Updates Window

Figure 20.3 Server Updates Window

This window allows the Administrator to "lock" the server. Locking the Server disconnects all connected clients, and prevents clients from connecting.

Locking the Server is usually done as part of the process of deploying a new update.

Lock / Unlock Updates Server
Use this control to lock the server before posting game updates to the update server. Unlock the Server to allow incoming client connections.

Logs
The Logs are a good place to find information about the Game Performance and any errors that might have occurred.

The logs can be found here:
<Realm Crafter Path>\<projectName>\Data\Logs\

Chapter 20: The Game Server

Four different logs can be used to analyze server activity.

- **Chat Log.txt** - This log contains entries for each chat message sent on the Server. New entries are appended to the end of the log.
- **Client Log.txt** - This log contains entries from the Client and might be useful in troubleshooting Client issues.
- **GUE Log.txt** - This log contains entries from the Game Editor and can be largely ignored.
- **Server Log.txt** - This log contains entries regarding the state of the Server. Errors in RC Scripts will be listed here, making this super-useful for troubleshooting scripts.

Deploying the Game Server and Updates

Deploying the Game Server

The Game Server can be deployed on the same network as the Game Client or on any computer that can access the Internet for wider distribution. Care needs to be taken to ensure that there is a clear connection between the Game Client and the Game server. That means computer firewalls need to be set to pass through the communications on whatever port you have defined on the Other Tab (the default is 25000) for both LAN and WAN hosting. In addition, if hosting by WAN, you will need an external IP address as well as to set your router to forward connections coming in for the Communications Port to the local IP address of your Game Server.

Deploying the Server to a LAN

The easiest way to deploy the Server is in a LAN configuration.

Choose a decent computer to run the Server on. It should have at least 4GB RAM and should have plenty of room on the hard drive to store all the database files associated with running the server and any custom scripts you have written. The Consumer / Prosumer level user will normally program using flat files (easiest) and the Pro user will more likely go for using a MySQL database to keep track of records.

The computer that you choose to be the server on your LAN must be on the same subnet as the Client computers.

The most common LAN configuration is for all the computers (Server AND Clients) to be on the same subnet, such as "192.168.1.x".

Chapter 20: The Game Server

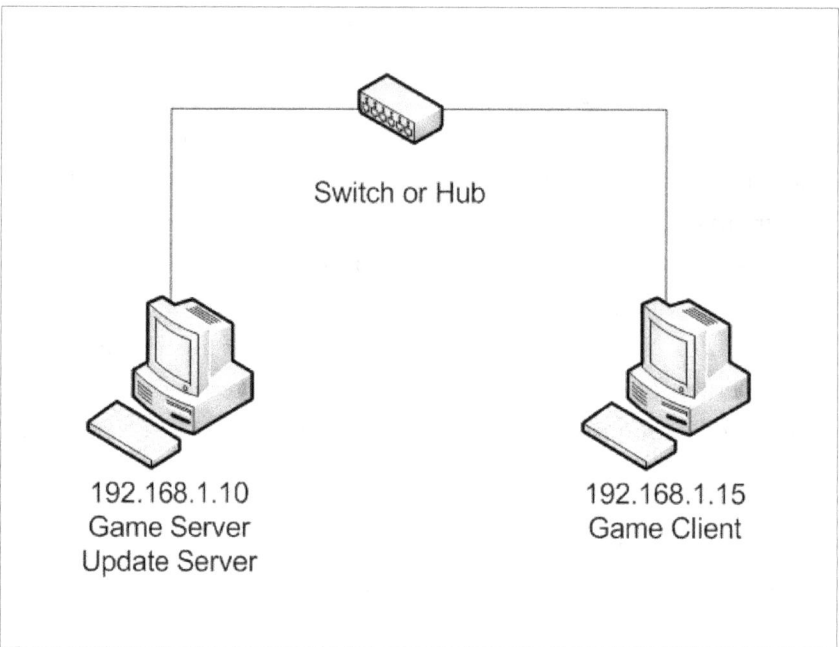

Figure 20.4 Typical Local Network Example

For this example, we are going to use the following assumptions:

- The LAN has 2 computers, the Server and Client.
- Both computers are on the same subnet.
- The IP address of the Game Server computer is 192.168.1.10
- The IP address of the Game Client is 192.168.1.15 but that is not relevant to the Game Server and is just for illustration purposes.

Be sure both computers can "see" each other on the network. One way this can be done is by sharing folders on each and then connecting to those folders from the other computer.

Once you have established that there is a clear and reliable connection between Client and Server computers, you are ready to deploy your game to the computers on the LAN.

When you have chosen a suitable computer to host the Game Server, it is time to generate the Game Server. Open up the Realm Crafter Game Editor and generate a Full Server (more info detailed in Chapter 3 under the Build Full Server section).

Next, we must tell the Game Client which computer to look to for a Server connection. This is done in the RCS Game Editor in the Other Tab.

Chapter 20: The Game Server

Enter the IP address of the server computer into the Host Name field. In this case, we enter 192.168.1.10. For now, leave the port number alone. The Port Number is the "channel" the server will use to communicate with the clients.

After making this change, switch to the Project Tab of the Game Editor and Build a Full Client. We want to include the test accounts we have been using, so answer "yes" when asked to include dynamic data.

Next, you are asked if you want to create a MySQL database. This is an advanced topic beyond the scope of this book. For now, answer "no".

The Server Program is then built and placed in folder called /server under <projectName>.

Copy the Server folder to the Server Computer and run the Server.exe program located inside the folder to start the Game Server. Unlock the Game Server using the Lock/Unlock button in the Server Updates window.

You are now ready to host your game.

Deploying the Server to a WAN

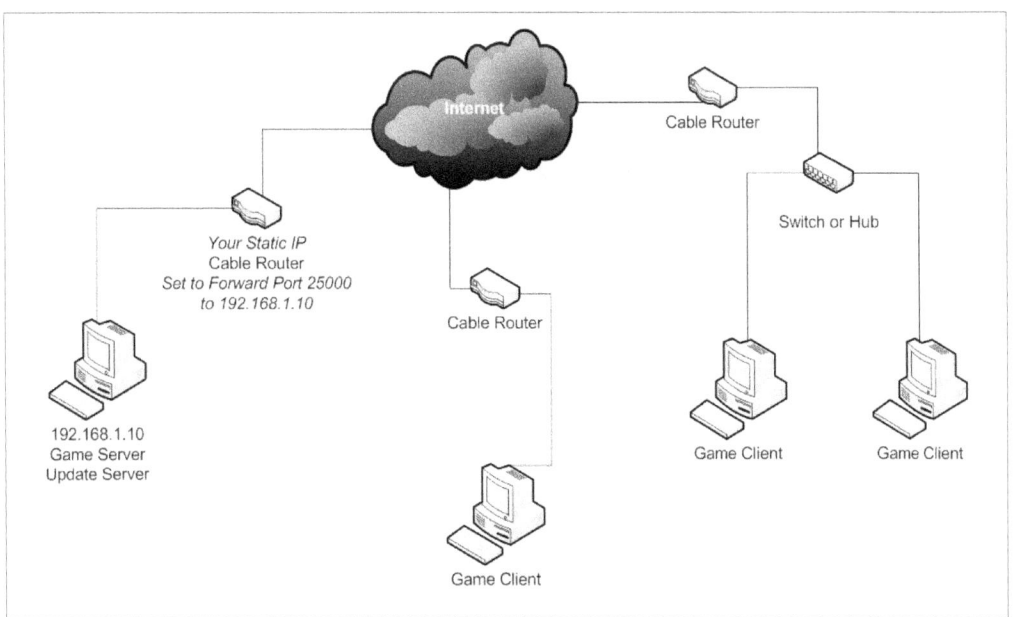

Figure 20.5 Typical WAN Scenario

Chapter 20: The Game Server

In order for Game Clients outside your network to link to your Game Server, it must be setup on a WAN (Wide Area Network). Instructions for setting up your game server on a WAN are the same as above, but you must also have an external IP address that clients outside your subnet can access. That usually means purchasing an IP address from your Internet Service Provider, and making sure your router is set to forward communications on the default RC Port (25000) to the internal IP address of the PC running the Game Server.

If your Internet Provider does not sell static IP addresses, it is possible to host a server using a dynamic IP address free. There are several third-party services available. Doing an Internet search for Free Dynamic DNS should get you started.

The IP addresses of the Game Clients are irrelevant to the Game Server.

Deploying Game Client Updates

The key to a successful game is ongoing development. From time to time, you will want to make updates to your Game World. Every good game needs new content to keep it fresh and interesting. Games also require occasional fixing. Maybe there is a place where players get stuck between pieces of scenery? Maybe you've added a new area, new monsters, new equipment, or new Quests.

If you are playing with friends on a local network, you can just give them copies of the game client; they don't need to run updates. However, if you are hosting a Game Server open outside your own local network, or you want to test the updater on your local network or host more than a few local clients, you will want to use the RC Patcher.

Using the Update Server, you can keep RC Clients synchronized with your current Game World using the automated RC Patcher located on a web server. When the Game Client is started, the RC Patcher will launch, show the latest news page, and download the current Game Client to the player's computer from a folder located on a web server using a PHP script. For this reason, the Update Files must be served from a web server that can run PHP. You can use a commercial web hosting service provider or you can host your own free web server using something like XAMPP.

For best results, try to host the Update Server on a different computer than the Game Server, otherwise clients connected to the Game Server would suffer lag every time a player connects for patching over the same Internet connection. For our simple example, the Game Server and Updates Server (Running XAMPP) are running on the same computer.

*Important: Make sure your new Game World is ready by editing the Language.txt file located in your Project Folder. You will want to change the values for GameName, Completed (the authors misspelled "Finished"), URL and News. This only needs to be done once per Project, not each time the Game Client is patched.

The line starting with URL= sets the web address of the update files for the RC Patcher.

In our Example, the Game Server is also running a XAMPP Web Server with a folder called "myRC" on the root level of the server (under htdocs). That folder

Chapter 20: The Game Server

contains a folder called "updates" which will be the repository for new Client Updates.

/myRC
    /news
        index.html
    /updates

Therefore URL = http://192.168.1.10/myRC/updates

The line starting with NEWS= sets the web address to the HTML file you want to be displayed in the RC Patcher. This is helpful for displaying patch notes, promotional info, a gateway to the game's website, and more.

Set NEWS= http://192.168.1.10/myRC/news/index.html

If you don't have a web page, you can just use a blank one as a placeholder, just be sure it's address matches what you have entered in the Language.txt file.

After this has been completed, you are ready to begin the update process.

The update process looks like this:

- **Create Client Patch Files**- These files will be uploaded to a web server so Game Clients could update with new content generated by the Publisher.

- **Lock the Update Server**- All Clients should be disconnected from the Game Server prior to posting the new update.

- **Copy Client Patch Files to the Server**- Patch files must be posted on the web server for Game Clients to access.

- **Unlock the Update Server**- Clients are now allowed to connect to the Game Server.

- **Provide New Game Client**- New users and existing users will need access to the full Game Client install, so make sure that is posted someplace new users can find it for download, or provide it on some sort of media.

This process may seem a little complicated, but after you have done it a few times, you'll find it can be executed quickly and is worth the time.

Creating Client Patch Files

The first step in creating a new Patch is to generate all the patch files Game Clients will need in order to update to the current version of your game.

When that is done, open the Game Editor and navigate to the Project Tab.

Choose Generate Client Update to build a new Full Client and a new Client Patch. Look in your Project Folder for the Game Client (/Game) and the new Client Patch (/Patches).

Lock the Update Server

Locking the Update Server forces all Game Clients to disconnect and puts the Game Server in Offline mode. This prevents having a mix of users with different content in their Game Client.

Keep an eye on the Accounts Roster to make sure all clients have been disconnected before continuing on to the next step.

Copy Client Patch Files to Server

The Patch Files must now be placed in the repository we indicated in the Language.txt file. Copy all the files from inside your local Project Folder/Patches/Files folder to the /updates folder on the Web Server. Be sure to copy the contents of the /Patches/Files folder, rather than the folder itself, to the repository destination.

In our Example, this would be to the myRc/updates folder located on our local XAMPP web server.

Unlock the Updates Server

The Update Server is now ready to serve updates to clients when they connect. Go to the Game Server and click Unlock Updates Server. Your Game Server is now set to Online and ready for incoming connections.

Chapter 20: The Game Server

Provide New Version

You have now setup a way for existing users to update the Game Client. It is also a good idea to make a full copy of the Game Client available for optional full download being sure to edit the Language.txt file located in the /Game folder so the Game Client knows where to get the Updates and News from. Change the game name as well).

Some games can be quite large and would take a long time to download. You can save time by distributing your game files on a DVD.

Glossary

1st Person View-
This is the view from the subject's perspective, as if viewing the world directly from their eyes. You can control which View Modes are available to the player using the Other Tab in the Game Editor.

3rd Person View-
This is the view from a perspective outside a subject's body. This is usually depicted as the point of view from a camera floating above and slightly behind the subject, though in most cases, the camera can be moved. You can control which View Modes are available to the player using the Other Tab in the Game Editor.

Actor-
Refers to the 3D representation of entities in the virtual game world. Actors are used for Players, NPC's, Monsters, or any other animated avatar in the game world. Any player- or computer-controlled entity in the game world that has a Life attribute or is animated is an Actor.

Alpha-
Refers to a grayscale overlay that controls the transparency of an underlying graphic. Black areas are transparent, white areas are opaque, and shades of gray are varying levels of opacity, according to how close to white or black they are.

Animation Set-
A collection of animations grouped by frames and given a label for each section of frames.

Armor-
Anything that can be used to protect an Actor from harm. Role-playing games usually have items that can give you some form of protection or another. Examples might be magic rings, thick leather jackets, mail coats, or even personal force fields.

Attribute-
In role-playing games, Attributes represent various aspects of a character's persona. Typical Attributes would include Strength, Life, Dexterity, and so forth.

Bones-
Underlying structure used to animate 3D meshes.

Glossary

Bounding Box-
This is the smallest cube that can encompass a 3D mesh.

Character Sheet-
The Character Sheet contains all the information on the Player Character's current condition. All the Attributes are listed on the Character Sheet, along with other relevant pieces of information, such as the character's name and profession.

Class-
Refers to a subset of a Race. This could be (Human) Wizards, (Orc) Warriors, (Martians) Pilots, (Robots) RepairBots, (Wild Animals) Lions, and so on. Think of Class as a Character's profession.

Game Client-
Refers to the game program and supporting files required to launch the game. This is what the player uses to link into the Game Server and play the game.

Client Update-
Refers to updated files required to be downloaded in order to provide updated Game Content to Game Clients.

Codec-
Stands for COder/DECcoder. This refers to the method used to encode media files into different formats, then to decode them back to native format used by the playback program.

Damage-
Anything that can hurt your character in the game world is said to cause "damage". Weapon strikes against you usually do some amount of damage, which is then reduced by your armor, and applied as a negative against the character's Life Points.

Emitter-
The point in space that particles are generated (spawned) from.

Equipped-
Refers to any items that are currently available for use by the character. When a character wields a sword or dons his armor, those items are considered "equipped".

Faction-
Any group of NPC's or Monsters that have something in common. It could be

something like a merchant guild, maybe a certain race, or hostile forest creatures. Increasing and decreasing Faction Rating over the course of the game increases and decreases that group's reaction with respect to the character.

Faction List-
This is the list of factions in the game and their relationship with respect to each other.

Force-
This is how the velocity direction and speed of a particle might be influenced by outside factors, such as wind or gravity.

Full Server-
Refers to the full set of files required to host the game world. Clients connect to the Server by some sort of network connection, by either LAN or WAN (Internet).

Game Editor (GE) -
The program used to create and edit a virtual game world using existing media assets. The Game Editor is the development environment used to create the virtual worlds that players move around and interact in.

Game Map-
Each Zone can have an associated map that is displayed when the Map Icon is clicked in the Game Client.

Grayscale-
Refers to a graphic made up of black, white, and shades of gray that is normally applied against another graphics file for a variety of effects and purposes, such as height maps and masks.

Gubbin-
Refers to a 3D mesh than can be mounted on the bones of another animated mesh and animated along with that bone. A gubbin could be a sword, shield, helmet, hat, shoulder guards, shin guards, etc.

Instance-
An instance is a unique copy (or iteration) of a Zone. Instances are used to keep separate copies of Zones. For instance, you may want a dungeon to only be used by members of a current group. You would use Instancing to allow a group into the dungeon, and then make a new instance of the dungeon for the next group to

Glossary

explore. Actors can be concurrently in different instances of the same Zone and cannot see or interact with one another.

Inventory-
This is a collection of in-game Items that the Character currently has in its possession. Inventory is usually kept in a container, such as a virtual backpack.

Item-
Refers to things the players can collect in the game world and use to interact with the game world. Common examples of Items would be potions, rings, tools, weapons, armor, and so forth. Items are normally listed in the Character's Inventory.

Mask-
Refers to transparency within a graphics file. Black areas of the mask are made transparent while white areas stay opaque. Masks are normally black and white and used for clipping, but can also be shades of gray when used for transparency.

Master Item List-
The list of all the Items available to players and NPC's in the game.

Media Library-
The collection of audio, textures, 3D meshes, and animated models that make up the content of the Project. The Game Editor can only use media contained in the Media Library. Media must be imported into the Media Library before use in the Game Editor. Every item in the Media Library has a unique ID number for reference within the Game Engine.

MMORPG (Massive Multiplayer Online Role Playing Game) -
Refers to an online game that features themed virtual worlds containing numerous players sharing the same server concurrently, interacting in real time. Players take on roles of fictitious characters and play out adventures within the context of the Game World.

Monster-
Refers to any game-controlled entity that opposes player-controlled characters. Usually refers to enemy combatants, but can also include non-combat NPC's.

Glossary

NPC- Non Player Character-
Refers to game entities that are not controlled by a player. This would include all the computer-controlled characters in a game.

Particle-
A graphic entity the size of a pixel that can be moved and manipulated automatically over time to achieve various effects, like sparks, or waterfalls. Particles can also have animated sprites connected to them that always face the camera, also known as "billboard" style. Particles are spawned, have a lifespan, then die and return to the particle pool.

Particle Lifespan-
This represents how long a particle sprite will last before it "dies" and disappears.

Particle Pool-
This is the number of available particles in the pool. When particles are spawned, they are removed from the Particle Pool, when they die, they return to the Particle Pool.

Project Manager (PM) -
The Realm Crafter Project Manger. This program allows the author to create new projects and manage existing ones.

Project Name-
This refers to the unique name (identifier) of a Project.

Project-
The collection of associated media files and program scripts which are required to implement a stand-alone virtual world.

Projectile-
Anything that can be used at a distance; a range weapon. Some examples of Projectiles could be arrows, slings stones, fireballs, grenades, etc.

Projectile List-
The Game Editor keeps a master list of projectile types. A projectile cannot be used unless it is present on this list.

Glossary

Race-
Refers to a top-level group of similar game entities. This could be Humans, Orcs, Martians, Robots, Wild Animals, and so forth.

RC Architect-
A program used for creating area interiors, such as dungeons, crypts, etc.

RC Gubbin Tool-
A program used to associate 3D meshes with Actor bones such that gear appears in the proper place on the Actor model when the item is equipped.

RC Rock Editor -
A program used to create low polygon rocks and boulders.

RC Terrain Editor-
A program used to create landscapes for use as areas or zones within the game.

RC Tree Editor-
A program used to create low-polygon trees that can sway in the wind and change color of the leaves as the seasons change.

RCS-
Realm Crafter Standard is the entry-level MMORPG Integrated Development Environment and game engine produced by Solstar.

Script Editor-
A program used to create programming scripts that allow customization of your game. Script Editors are usually just fancy text editors.

Skill-
Characters can have Skills that indicate how good they are at certain tasks. Usually the higher the Skill, the better the Character is at performing tasks with that Skill. Skills could be things such as Lock Picking, heavy Weapons, Setting Traps, Accuracy, and so forth.

Test Client-
A program used to test games during development. The Test Server must be running and unlocked before the Test Client is launched.

Glossary

Test Server-
A program used to test games during development. The Test Client must be run with the Test Server.

Texture-
Refers to a graphic that is used as a skin over 3D meshes.

Trap-
Refers to unseen or unobvious pitfalls, poison needles, toxic gases, and other nasty things that make player's lives more interesting.

Velocity-
This represents an object's speed through space. The higher the velocity, the farther the difference between rendered frames, the lower the velocity, the less the distance traveled, and the less difference between rendered frames.

Weapon-
Anything that can be used in a fight. Role-playing games feature ways you can protect yourself against in-game Monsters, NPC's, and even other players. Weapons typically come in the form of crossbows and swords, but could be anything you can imagine.

Weather-
Refers to rain, snow, fog, and other environmental qualities present in the local area.

X Axis-
In 3D space, the X axis runs left and right. Increasing the value of X moves objects to the right, decreasing X moves objects to the left. The X axis is perpendicular to the Z axis.

Y Axis-
In 3D space, the Y axis runs up and down. Increasing the value of Y moves objects up, decreasing Y moves objects down.

Z Axis-
In 3D space, the Z axis runs straight out of the screen. Increasing the value of Z moves objects towards you, decreasing Z moves objects away from you. The Z axis is perpendicular to the X axis.

Glossary

Zone-

A Zone represents a physical location within the Game World. A zone can be as small as a jail cell or as large as a continent. Castles, dungeons, forests, mountains, cellars, stables, spaceships, and taverns are all examples of possible Zones.

Appendix A: Updater Language.txt

Located at /projectName/Language.txt (note: "Finnished" is misspelled):

GameName = My Game

OverallProgress = Overall Progress

Quit = Close

Play = Start!

Checking = Checking Files...

Downloading = Downloading Files...

Final = Updating Files...

Completed = Finnished! Press Start!

ExitTitle = Exit

ExitText = Are you sure you want to quit?

Application = Game.exe

URL=http://www.solstargames.net/MyRCGameUpdates

News=http://www.solstargames.net/MyRCGameNews.html

www.ingramcontent.com/pod-product-compliance
Lightning Source LLC
Chambersburg PA
CBHW080909170526
45158CB00008B/2051